CW01022180

Targeted Prayer

A Guide to Help Get Answers

ROGER GRASSHAM

malcolm down

PUBLISHING

First published 2021 by Malcolm Down Publishing Ltd.
www.malcolmdown.co.uk

24 23 22 21   7 6 5 4 3 2 1

British Library Cataloguing in Publication Data
A catalogue record for this book is available from the British Library.

ISBN 978-1-912863-74-7

Endorsements

At some point every one of us will have felt what the first disciples felt when, seeing and hearing Jesus pray, they asking him to teach them how to pray.

How can we make prayer a living and dynamic part of our everyday relationship with Jesus – to literally walk and talk with him and see the transformative power of answered prayer?

I love that *Targeted Prayer* flows out of Roger's experience of rooting prayer in real-life relationship with Christ. In an honest, accessible, and really practical way, this book will encourage and enable you to pray with greater faith, focus and effectiveness.

Chris Cartwright, General Superintendent, Elim Pentecostal Church

I have had the privilege of knowing Roger for a number of years. He lives what he preaches, and in this case, what he has written. His book *Targeted Prayer* flows out of a deep well of personal relationship with the Holy Spirit. But Roger's book is not only inspirational, challenging, and encouraging, it is above all practical, giving each of us hands-on 'prayer guides' that help every believer, regardless of our level of experience and maturity, to start praying, and seeing results. I encourage every believer, and every Christian leader to read, and apply the powerful truths presented in *Targeted Prayer* and see kingdom breakthrough in our generation.

Jonathan Conrathe, Founder and Lead Evangelist, Mission24

It is sincerely a delight for me to write a recommendation for Roger's book re: prayer guides. My main reason is much more than the content and wisdom, but because I know the man. Having ministered some forty years across many nations, I have met many ministers and pastors and learned much about God's people in general. Yet any veteran minister will understand what I mean when I say it's always a blessing to find a 'real one'. Roger is one of the real men of God. He carries the wisdom, and scars, of what it means to give your life for the good of others, as Jesus did. In Scripture we know the verse that tells us Jesus 'esteemed others more than himself' and 'gave no thought to his own interests' (see Philippians 2:3-4). This is very visible in Roger's life. Also, the key and most vital badge of a follower of Jesus is upon him: humility. I've never heard Roger ever speak ill of anyone, or seen anger overcome him, but what I have seen again and again is his utter willingness to sacrifice his own time and being for the good of others. This is why I'm happy to recommend this book. I know this man. He is one of the real ones. Father smiles at his name. Everything in this book comes from a heart that wants to help people grow in Christ. He cares nothing for personal recognition. I truly enjoyed and found wisdom in his writings, and I know you will as well. Please take advantage of this work of heaven. It will serve to not only motivate prayer, but initiate a far stronger sense of God's presence within your lives and churches.

Rod Anderson, Senior Pastor, Commonwealth Church and Joint Founder of The Prayer Foundation

I would like to fully endorse this excellent publication written by my good friend and colleague Roger Grassham, and members of the national prayer team of the Elim Pentecostal Churches. This material flows from the hearts and lives of wise, seasoned practitioners in prayer ministry, and will serve to be a powerful resource both for church prayer groups, and personal intercession. The purpose of *Targeted Prayer* is to equip, encourage, and enable prayer to be effective. I warmly commend it.

Alistair Cole, Chair, National Prayer Network of the Elim Churches 2005-2018; Director, The Watchman Ministries

One of the great mysteries of the Christian life is the power and mechanism of prayer. The notion that we can kneel next to our bed and change things happening on the other side of the world in real time is mind-warping. The author is challenging us to take the leap of faith to discover the intrinsic power of answered prayer through specific requests to God. I suggest you jump in feet first!

Jonathan Oloyede, National Day of Prayer and Worship

Church leaders excel in preaching 'you should' sermons on prayer – and it is certainly true we should all pray more. What *Targeted Prayer* does is to answer the question the disciples posed to Jesus: 'How should' we pray? Well-researched, biblically based and abounding in the rich pastoral depth that the author possesses, this book is essential reading for anyone committed to prevailing prayer. I wholeheartedly recommend it to you.

John Glass, General Superintendent, Elim churches (2000-2016), Chair of Council, Evangelical Alliance (2014-2018)

This is a well-written and comprehensive resource for those looking for tools to enhance their prayer life. Roger Grassham underpins key guidelines with personal experience, conveying his passion for engaging in intimacy with God, and as such, expresses prayer as a lifestyle built on and developed over time through commitment and encounter. His many testimonies bear witness to this, always giving God the glory. He writes, therefore, not as a theorist but as a practitioner, and these guidelines are born out of his own experience, coupled with the rich veins of resources drawn from engaging with others within the Church in this essential ministry.

The well-laid structures act like road signs and pointers along the pathways we tread in our daily walk of discipleship, highlighting different approaches to varying prayer situations and needs, whilst bringing clarity and understanding. It is a good reference book to dip into, refer to and seek direction from, covering a wide range of areas and aspects to enhance our engagement with God, both as individuals and corporately, as the body of Christ."

Henry Pradella, retired Anglican minister, author and former secondary teacher

Over many years I've had the privilege of serving with Roger in various areas of prayer. His integrity, wisdom and experience have been invaluable to me as I have navigated leading prayer personally, in local church and on a national scale. With insight, information and inspiration this book will be a resource to you. It will encourage you to pray and lead prayer with fresh strategy and confidence. I highly recommend Roger and this book to you. May you discover more deeply the invitation to partner with God's kingdom purposes through prayer.

Sarah Whittleston, National Prayer Director for Elim Prayer and Co-Lead Pastor, Elim Life Church, Kingstanding

Having stood and knelt with Roger over many years in Canning Town and the wider community, I know that he has lived out all that he writes in this book. It is a very valuable tool for any individual, group or church seeking to build their own relationship with God and be faithful and effective in wanting God's kingdom to come and his will done in all areas of our local, national and international communities' life.

Peter Watherston, Anglican minister of Mayflower Family Centre 1982-1996 and Chair of Transform Newham 2002-2013

Prayer is the very life breath of a Christian, yet an area in which we often feel so challenged. I am strangely encouraged that at least twice the disciples asked Jesus to teach them to pray (Matthew 6:9-13; Luke 11:2-4) near the beginning of His ministry and years later towards the end. He answers both with the Lord's Prayer; we are all still in Prayer 101.

In this book, Roger Grassham doesn't just explain the theory of prayer but gives practical tools for effective personal and corporate prayer. I know Roger to be more than the great teacher he is on prayer, but also that he has been a faithful practitioner for many years. I commend him and this book to you.

David Campbell, member of National Leadership Team, Elim Pentecostal Churches

As a believer in the inspirational and practical gospel of Christ and as a businessman in the City of London, I have no doubt that God loves to answer authentic and heartfelt prayers – 'if our hearts do not condemn us, we have confidence before God' (1 John 3:21). How amazing is that!?

Having journeyed with Roger Grassham for more than fifteen years in the City, I have found him to be a true worshipper, a man seeking God's heart whether playing a guitar or leading a business meeting. Be blessed by his godly wisdom.

Paul Szkiler, Founder of A Call to Business and CEO of Truestone Impact Investment Management Limited

In spiritual warfare, the Word of God is 'the sword of the spirit' (Ephesians 6:17), so I imagine prayer as the bow and arrow. God's overarching grace causes the challenges in our lives to launch the cry of our heart as an arrow of truth. Often aimed into a specific situation, but always going via the heart of God! The arrowhead, a *Rhema* word hewn from the same refined steel as the *Logos* sword. Light and sharp to focus on its purpose, rather than inflated with vain words to tingle people's ears. The shaft of organic wood, straight-talking passionate humanity. The Trinitarian feathers, gently guiding to its target – straight and true!

I met Roger nearly fifteen years ago when, by God-instance, a developer appointed me to assist them in helping the church that Roger was leading. It was the start of a long friendship which has been a continual source of great blessing to me. During this time, I have seen Roger and Ros up close and can recommend them to you as passionate, prophetic people full of prayer and praise, always displaying the loving pastoral heart of Jesus.

Roger sets out his stall in the opening quote from our friend, Jonathan Oloyede – 'Christian prayer … is always relational'. Our God lovingly invites us into his presence in the throneroom of decision, not to be a passive observer but a significant influencer in the outcome through intercession. Our Creator invites us to take up responsibility again by making us response-able through prayer. Our Father invites us to deepen our relationship by experiencing his heart on a matter, to move it, and as maturing children, to learn the Family business. Roger provides helpful advice and practical guidance in these 'How to' guides, whether you are just starting or are well underway on this path of encountering our Father's heart, mind and word through prayer.

Gareth Gerner, Senior Partner at Arc Design Partnership LLP and Director IXO (Consulting) LLP

How I wish I had had this prayer book at the start of my ministry. In this book are pearls of wisdom only gleaned through toiling on the master's harvest field. I would encourage all Christians to read this book, especially those who have a care and responsibility to care for others in community or groups. Just brilliant a must for anyone seeking to dig deeper in prayer.

Yinka Oyekan
President of the Baptist Union of Great Britain (2020-2021)

The distinctive about Christian prayer is that it is always relational – it takes place in the context of a loving relationship between God and us – and just as there are many forms of expression within a loving relationship between two human beings, so there are many ways to communicate in our relationship with God.

Jonathan Oloyede[1]

Prayer is a privilege. God invites us to partner with him in his kingdom purpose and plans.

Sarah Whittleston[2]

We must remember that the goal of prayer is the ear of God. Unless that is gained the prayer has utterly failed.

E.M. Bounds[3]

God wants to purify our minds until we can bear all things, believe all things, hope all things, and endure all things. God dwells in you, but you cannot have this divine power until you live and walk in the Holy Ghost, until the power of the new life is greater than the old life.

Smith Wigglesworth[4]

Let us resolve to be part of the great prayer army that God is building from every nation and every stream and tradition. God will always respond to the cry of His people…

Alistair Cole[5]

The evidence of the early Church is that their patterns of life included 'prayers' – not perfunctory religious ritual, but the natural life-flow of people who were learning to pray.

Jack Hayford[6]

Acknowledgements

My best friend and soul mate, Ros, has been an amazing companion in faith for more than forty-seven years, thus far, and we have been married for forty-five of those. Ros is a very special person who has been my wife, mother to our grown-up children and also a grandmother. During more than forty years of bi-vocational and full-time pastoral ministry, Ros has been a spiritual mother and friend to many people, bringing wisdom and prophetic insight, which has caused people to grow and mature in the faith. I will be forever grateful to God for finding me the right person to spend all these years together, and counting.

I am enormously grateful to a number of special people who have helped me with the production of this book. It is fair to say that the wonderful Elim Prayer team, of which I have been a part for more than ten years, have to take a lot of credit for the concepts included within this prayer guide. What I hadn't expected was to be the person that God would use to design the layout and then write the text. When 1 Corinthians 1:27 speaks about God using the 'foolish things of the world to shame the wise', it is definitely true, and what you will be reading is the proof of this.

One special member of the Elim Prayer team is Rev June Freudenberg. She has patiently read every one of the Prayer Guides and carefully edited them, while checking theology, context and phraseology along the way. Sections 4, 5 and 6 have been drawn from material that June has produced in the past, which I have added to, and which is included with her permission. It has been an absolute pleasure for me to draw from June's many years' experience of pastoral and grief counselling knowledge and prayer/Bible teaching background. June was a valued minister and part of the leadership team at Kensington Temple for many years. In addition, June has been an integral part of the Prayer for Parliament team, representing the Elim Pentecostal Church in that capacity, and having a strong prophetic and prayerful influence while serving God in praying for our national governmental leaders.

I would like to thank the current Elim Prayer team leader Rev Sarah Whittleston, with whom it is a privilege to work, together with all the other wonderful ministerial colleagues who make up the national core group that promotes life-transforming prayer in the Elim churches. The encouragement and support has been fantastic and their passion and commitment to all things prayer is second to none.

One of the people quoted in this book, and whose own book on prayer is recommended at the end, is Rev Alistair Cole. It was he who first invited me to join the then Elim prayer network group more than ten years ago. Thank you, Alistair, for all you have and are doing for the kingdom to 'teach, watch and pray'.[7]

Other influences on prayer have been pastors Rod and Julie Anderson,[8] who are the leaders of Commonwealth Church in the West End of London and have also been faithful to the ministry of prayer and the prophetic through The Prayer Foundation (part of their overall ministry). Your teaching and influence on our lives has been immense, more than you realise, and much of the faith-filled teaching, mentoring and guidance has been foundational in the ongoing realm of ministry.

There are others who have had strong prayerful influence and it would be remiss of me not to mention the late pastor John Barr, with whom I had the enormous honour to work, during the 1980s and 1990s. He was my friend, pastor, mentor and inspiration, like he was for so many others who knew him. A genuine twentieth-century prophet who was highly respected across all Church denominations.

His prophetic insight and extraordinary ministry changed so many people's lives, including my own. Much of what I live out today in prayer was nurtured during those years of observing, listening and teaching.

In relation to other groups of people I had amazing prayer encounters with are River Church in east London, where I ministered as senior pastor for seventeen years. I have several decades of participation in prayer with Transform Newham (united churches prayer in east London). During this time in the borough, the Global Day of Prayer initiative was birthed while I was a fellow trustee together with Dr Jonathan Oloyede. The times of prayer in stadiums and regular weekly early mornings with fellow ministers from across the borough have left a significant imprint on me.

I'd like to thank Paul Szkiler for the amazing opportunities to worship, pray and release the prophetic with A Call to Business in the City of London. The experience of worship leading, praying and ministering in the heart of the Square Mile was a huge influence and was partly responsible for me seeing that everyone can be a minister in their workplace.

Finally, I'm enormously grateful to Sheila Jacobs who has edited this book. She is an established author and freelance editor in her own right. Her critical eye and attention to detail have been invaluable in getting the material you are about to read into the best shape possible. Her spiritual insight and expertise combined have given me the encouragement needed to be a finisher and not just a starter. Thank you.

Contents

Contents

Foreword

I learned to pray from an incredibly early age, growing up in a family that regularly attended a Salvation Army church in the north of England, attending the services every week. From my earliest memory, I was encouraged to pray every night for family and our immediate needs while on my knees beside the bed. At the age of six I realised how wayward I was being, and realised I needed to change. With help by mature Christians, I was led to pray and ask God's forgiveness for my sin, and then accept Jesus as my Lord and Saviour, by faith. After I had done this, I knew something had happened. Why? Because my conscience became extremely sensitive. I always had a sense of conviction when I had done anything wrong. In fact, my mother used to say I could not tell a lie and get away with it because she could read it in my face!

I grew up and became very musical, playing brass instruments, and I became very accomplished. I practised daily, and was totally absorbed by the band and orchestras I was a part of. I was also a very competent singer. My mum entered me into an annual music festival, where I won prizes and did very well. As a side interest I taught myself how to play the guitar, something that would become important to me later. However, my pride in my ability was a mask for what was going on inside.

The music-making became my 'God' and over a period of years during my teens and early twenties I didn't live for God, and became a hypocrite. I was outwardly spiritual and participating in the church service activity, but inwardly a dry shell, doing everything in my own strength. My daily encounters with God were reduced as I forged my own path. This is significant, because I failed at pretty much everything academic, whilst focusing efforts on music.

I was drained and empty, had been enticed onto a path that was about 'me', and God had to take a back seat. In essence, I walked away from him. However, although I had abandoned God, God had not abandoned me. In my heart of hearts, I was searching for a greater depth of truth, and I looked into a range of different realms of spirituality that sent me up a cul-de-sac. What I discovered was that God was there, waiting for me. I had become low, depressed, fearing failure and bereft of clear direction in life, spiritually.

What was happening to me was no surprise to God, but it was a surprise to me! I started a search for more truth and understanding of spiritual things. The intensity of my enquiring mind and soul moved me into a young people's Bible study group. I gave the young lady leading the group an awfully hard time with my questions. She invited me to join an adult Bible study group for Christians of all denominations. The leaders, Anglican curates at the time, and who became long-time friends and mentors, could see how spiritually hungry I was and encouraged me to study and ask questions. The group was studying the Gospel of John and after quite a few months, had reached chapter 15. I realised I was not bearing fruit, and what was there had shrivelled up. I felt dreadful, empty and a complete fraud; the Word of God began to come alive in me by the Holy Spirit.

I had by then started to use my guitar much more, and invariably led worship at the Bible study group, learning the new songs that formed part of the charismatic movement in the 1960s and 1970s.

Soon, my newly found Christian leader friends led me in prayers of repentance and laid hands on me to receive the baptism of the Holy Spirit. This was the same experience that Jesus' disciples had on the day of Pentecost:

When the day of Pentecost came, they were all together in one place. Suddenly a sound like the blowing of a violent wind came from heaven and filled the whole house where they were sitting. They saw what seemed to be tongues of fire that separated and came to rest on each of them. All of them were filled with the Holy Spirit and began to speak in other tongues as the Spirit enabled them.

(Acts 2:1-4)

That night as I lay on my bed, I had not spoken in tongues, but I had the most astonishing peace overwhelm me. The sense of God's presence and peace immediately drove away every fear and sense of failure I had had.

I experienced this nightly for a period of six months. Soon after, the first major manifestation of God's power and anointing became evident. This was particularly so when I prayed out loud in the church meetings; things happened within the congregation – both positive and negative.

When I shared testimony about my new, intimate relationship with Jesus, it was like an artesian well of energy that gushed out from my spirit. Some people were overwhelmed and offended that I spoke about Jesus much more than I used to. In fact, the change in me seemed to make a lot of people very uncomfortable. I felt God speak to me about my priorities, so much so that I decided that I had to lay my music on the altar, so to speak, and therefore stopped the brass-playing side of my church involvement because it had stolen my heart, and subsequently had too much influence on me.

Some weeks after my initial release in the power of the Holy Spirit, I received the gift of tongues:

to another faith by the same Spirit, to another gifts of healing by that one Spirit, to another miraculous powers, to another prophecy, to another distinguishing between spirits, to another

speaking in different kinds of tongues, and to still another the interpretation of tongues.
(1 Corinthians 12:9-10)

This has subsequently become something that has become a vital part of my prayer life to this day. In the weeks and months that followed, prayer, the Scriptures and fellowship became my priority. All the idolatry of music-making for its own sake, had died within me. One thing that remained musically was the area that had been originally less important, the guitar-playing. Now, that skill was to be use solely for worship and a tool for developing an intimate sense of God's presence.

The young lady who fielded all my questions at the young people's Bible study and had introduced me to her Holy Spirit-filled friends, soon became incredibly special to me. Surprise, surprise, she is now my wife! I will be forever grateful to God for this.

After the events described above, I assisted in taking a group of young people away on a 'Teens and Twenties' weekend with the Good News Crusade evangelistic ministry run by Don Double in Cornwall. During these few days, not only did some of the young people have a significant encounter with God, but so did I! I received a direct call to prayer and intercession which I took very seriously. In the weeks that followed I began to arise at 6 a.m. every day, read the Bible and spend time in prayer. This continued for more than three years, and to this day early morning is a good time for me to be reading God's Word, starting the day in God's presence.

There is so much more of my testimony that illustrates the leading of God. Suffice to say at this point, Ros and I moved on to new churches in a transitional season, and eventually I went on to become a church leader and pastor. During the journey I met and became best friends with the late pastor John Barr.[9] He asked me to come and take a 'Macedonian call'[10] to come and help him in Canning Town. Subsequently, he discipled me and showed, among many other things, just me how influential prayer and listening to the Holy Spirit can be in church life.

I remained bi-vocational as a senior manager in local authority direct services and a civil engineer, while also in church leadership in east London for twenty years before going the traditional 'full-time' route. During all those years of learning, watching and serving, I discovered how to pray effectively in the power of the Holy Spirit. I found ways to do this in my mind during challenging business meetings, to pray in the spirit quietly when faced with complicated relationship challenges, and to pray aloud authoritatively in the face of spiritual challenge.

I have attended and led thousands of prayer meetings large and small, and hope to continue to do so all the while I am able. Prayer is a lifestyle, not just something that we do. Jesus taught us how to pray when he gave us the Lord's Prayer[11] but for disciples, that should be just the start. I want to be like Jesus and serve God, but also make sure I give priority to times aside to wait on God and pray. Listening is just as important as speaking to God. I am constantly surprised by how God speaks to my heart when I give him the time and space to do so. I have discovered that listening to God points us in the right direction towards praying prayers that get answers.

During the decades of leadership and pastoral ministry, I have discovered that prayer is not something we just do when things are not going the way we would like them to. In some ways, prayer is like a bank account that needs to be credited regularly so that we have enough when expensive challenges come. This is not a perfect analogy, but our prayer life is something that needs to be kept in credit and not allowed to require an overdraft where we use someone else's funds to get by! The lifestyle of prayer means that we pray continuously, as 1 Thessalonians 5:17 tells us. How have I done that over the years? By having regular conversations with God between things that I do; by always asking God to ensure that I give the right emphasis at the next meeting; by asking God for wisdom when I know things are going to be challenging. Two more things. Firstly, I have followed a consistent pattern of praying in the Spirit using the language that was released to me when I was baptised in the Holy Spirit.[12] Sometimes we need to pray in an unknown tongue, because we do not know how to pray with normal words; also, so that we pray prayers that get answers and that are in the flow of God's will and purpose for our lives and those that we serve and lead. Secondly, I have needed to learn to pray with an open mind and heart to God, and not with my mind already made up. This has saved me from huge disappointments and disillusionment. We need to let God be God when we pray!

I have found that if we don't let go, then we end up inadvertently controlling situations, and when we do so, we need to continue this in order to perpetuate the direction and decisions that ensue. I absolutely need to pray with an open heart and mind that has been quietened, ensuring that scripture is the 'lamp for my feet' and 'light on my path' (Psalm 119:105) and allowing the Holy Spirit to illuminate God's Word, showing me how to apply it practically.

These prayer guides and underlying principles are, to a large degree, the outworking of life principles and a lengthy journey of listening, learning, yielding, bending the knee, allowing God to speak prophetically and submission to his will.

Over the last forty years or so, I have discovered a direct link in prayer between three key areas:

1. Worship
2. Prayer
3. Prophetic

Each of these three areas are expressions of adoration, communication and spontaneity of the Spirit which will usher in the heart of God, his presence and opportunity for deep encounter with him. When we combine all three together, there is a trinity of giftings and ministries at work, and they must always be undergirded by truths that are found in Scripture. These areas combined facilitate heaven's melodies, the cry and groanings of the human heart, and ears attuned to our heavenly Father for 'now words' that bring revelation and challenge. I have seen lives changed, amazing situations transformed and powerful people change their minds simply because we prayed, worshipped, and prophesied as the Holy Spirit led. I have encountered spiritual battles and challenges that only prayer could have broken, and many times it did.

I love the presence of God. Let us all attune our hearts and give him the time and space to move in and through us as we pray.

I commend these prayer guides to you. They are preceded by some generic principles that I have adopted and that are foundational to effective prayer. Be blessed as you read and be fruitful as you pray using the tools within these pages.

Roger Grassham

The Prayer Conversation

What is prayer?

I believe that prayer is a lifestyle and not just a ritual or something part of Church liturgy. It is a conversation with the living God, just as you talk to a close friend or member of family. I believe that God does not differentiate between a Christian and non-Christian when it comes to prayer. He hears any cry of the heart, and prayer is a way to communicate with him. When people say to me, I am not sure how to pray, I tell them to imagine they are just like the two disciples walking along the road to Emmaus in Luke 24 with Jesus by their side. It was a shared experience for them, talking and listening, and it can be the same for us now. Our God is never far away, and he loves to spend time with us, especially to receive our adoration and worship. Therein lies a real key, that prayer and worship are entwined together. When we tune our hearts into God by the power of the Holy Spirit, prayer and worship become a dynamic pairing that can prophetically release us into an intimate place with God that plugs us into a divine current to pray prayers that get answers.

It is not an exact science. There are many ways to pray, which sometimes lead to periods of silence where we listen to and not just talk to our living God.

What is this book about?

This is one book about prayer, but with many parts. You can read it as a whole or selectively pick out a subject for prayer that you want to focus on, or have specific interest in. It is predominantly designed to be a 'handbook' for those who want to become more focused in prayer and intercessory at a deeper level (interrogating and listening to God).

The material presented within each prayer guide should help you to develop a deeper understanding of the subject matter as an aid to more effective prayer. It will help you to have a sharper spiritual eye into the background detail of the subject, thus ensuring greater accuracy and historic understanding.

The material that is presented in each guide should help you pray more consistently and learn how to ask questions of God, having researched background, history and the context of the specific subject matter. The subject prayer guides are a starting point, but you can add local information that you are aware of.

This is not a book of stories, although there are some testimonies; the title gives a pretty clear indication that it contains. Writing prayer guides was an idea birthed by a team of devoted prayer warriors, who are themselves leaders within their churches. They all have a passion and deep desire is to equip the Church to engage in, and be passionate about, prayer in all its forms. Over a two-year period the idea became a focused project to equip the Church of Jesus Christ to engage in fervent, effectual prayers that get answers. Practically, it became evident that the writing of the prayer guides needed consistency and clarity in presentation, and therefore was best written by one person from the group.

This is a book that will help give shape to a focused prayer subject, and can be used by individuals, groups, or a whole church. By using the prayer guides, the person or group of people can intercede knowing more information about a particular subject. The prayer guides help to scratch below the surface to find valuable, informative background and scriptural foundation. The prayer guides have a consistent format that helps to bring structure to the time spent with the subject.

This book is a tool that helps to focus on prayer, and see that targeted prayer gets targeted answers! Hopefully, the prayer guides will help the reader to be specific. Sometimes people pray what I call 'all round the world' prayers, trying to catch every need they are aware of. There is nothing wrong with praying about everything that comes to mind; God hears all our prayers. However, I have discovered that clear, targeted, focused and specific prayer gets the best results. Here, there is clear encouragement not to ramble. The way the prayer guides have been written give plenty of scope for creativity on a specific subject, which means you become more informed, thorough and knowledgeable about that subject, thus helping you to empathise and gain deeper understanding.

Engaging

Engaging in prayer is about engaging with God. Our relationship with God starts with God loving us as we see in the Gospel stories, and we respond to his love and are transformed by him. This is a two-way relationship that needs cultivating regularly, in the same way that we build relationships in general, and in and around our churches. Building the foundations of a loving, responsive and long-lasting relationship takes time and focus. I[13] trust that these guides will help people build on what already exists, and further develop and deepen understanding and expectation of God, who desires to answer our prayers.

I want to see people engaging in prayer using these guides and thus bring a multiplication in the release of creativity and God-given insights through prayer. Also, it would be great to see an exponential level of understanding and release of the Holy Spirit's anointing and gifts as we pray. In addition, why shouldn't you and your church be in the vanguard of hearing God prophetically as people pray individually as well as corporately. I believe we are called to watch and pray consistently (1 Peter 5:8). Together we can all make a difference in our nation and the nations of the world.

Who is it for?

It can be used by individuals, small groups, or churches. You will notice that the prayers are written in the plural, but can be adapted for individual use. My goal has always been to provide a useful resource that will help equip people with additional tools to pray effectively and with great creativity. It is likely that small groups and churches already adopt similar guidance, but if not, I hope the information will bring greater stimulus to more effective praying.

1. Principles of Prayer

In writing the prayer guides and providing some explanatory principles, it has been my desire to encourage readers to develop the understanding that prayer is a lifestyle and not just something that we do. It is my sincere hope that the following principles will encourage a greater fluency and articulation of prayer for all the Church family. Stop, look and listen to what God is saying could be something you do for each of the following.

- **Principle 1: Focusing our mind and heart on God** is more important than the people around us. Even so we need to be sensitive to the group in a collaborative way. This helps to remove a level of self-consciousness and nervousness about praying aloud. Look to Jesus. This verse says Jesus was 'resolute' in his goal! Let us follow his example and be resolute in our prayers:

As the time approached for him to be taken up to heaven, Jesus resolutely set out for Jerusalem.
(Luke 9:51)

- **Principle 2: The enemy of our souls** (Satan) (Ephesians 6:12) wants to distract us and fill our minds with thoughts and emotions about other things. We need to take captive these thoughts and be alert to the devil's strategies. This scripture urges us to demolish arguments:

We demolish arguments and every pretension that sets itself up against the knowledge of God, and we take captive every thought to make it obedient to Christ.
(2 Corinthians 10:5)

- **Principle 3: Listening to God is as important as talking to him.** Taking time for God to speak to us will help us be focused in prayer. Let us be like Samuel:

The LORD came and stood there, calling as at the other times, 'Samuel! Samuel!' Then Samuel said, 'Speak, for your servant is listening.'
(1 Samuel 3:10)

- **Principle 4: As we dwell in God's presence**, we should let our spiritual creativity flourish, but be anchored in God's Word and sound doctrinal teaching:

Your word is a lamp for my feet, a light on my path.
(Psalm 119:105)

- **Principle 5: Whichever topic we are led to pray for**, we need to be positive and have an emphasis on 'Praying thoughtfully and carefully' rather than 'Praying controllingly'. By doing this we are consistently wanting to see the very best outcomes for people, and allowing God to act in accordance with his will and purpose:

give thanks in all circumstances; for this is God's will for you in Christ Jesus.
(1 Thessalonians 5:18)

- **Principle 6: It is alright to structure our prayers in a liturgical way**, but we should always be led by the Holy Spirit and pray constructively:

And pray in the Spirit on all occasions with all kinds of prayers and requests. With this in mind, be alert and always keep on praying for all the Lord's people.
(Ephesians 6:18)

- **Principle 7: Be discerning when seeking God in prayer**, and be led by the Holy Spirit. This will increase the influence and impact of our prayers. Learning to listen to God as well as talk to God will enable us to hear the prompting of the Holy Spirit more clearly. Then we can pray more effectively, and with more wisdom:

If any of you lacks wisdom, you should ask God, who gives generously to all without finding fault, and it will be given to you. But when you ask, you must believe and not doubt, because the one who doubts is like a wave of the sea, blown and tossed by the wind. That person should not expect to receive anything from the Lord. Such a person is double-minded and unstable in all they do.
(James 1:5-8)

- **Principle 8: God is creative**, and he has made us creative, so be open to the idea of setting out a prayer room in Zones and Stations to pray. These areas can be created during specific seasons of prayer in our churches. By doing this alongside the other Principles outlined, it will help facilitate prayer that is transformational and that gets answers. Having areas that are focused will enable us to target our prayers more effectively.

If you remain in me and my words remain in you, ask whatever you wish, and it will be done for you.
(John 15:7)

- **Principle 9: Regular, effective and focused prayer** is to be seen as an urgent and compelling request of Scripture and should be seen as an imperative of prayer. An example of this for government and authorities is:

I urge, then, first of all, that petitions, prayers, intercession and thanksgiving be made for all people--for kings and all those in authority, that we may live peaceful and quiet lives in all godliness and holiness.'
(1 Timothy 2:1-2)

- **Principle 10: The best kind of 'Engage' prayer** is when church people have a strong relationship with and know the people and community being prayed for. This becomes more personal and is more likely to encourage ownership by our people as they identify with the people and the needs around them.

Therefore confess your sins to each other and pray for each other so that you may be healed. The prayer of a righteous person is powerful and effective.
(James 5:16)

- **Principle 11: Aligning our prayers with heaven** will enable us to identify God's assignments on earth. To do this, a divine connection in prayer and intercession out of our regular relationship with God will establish a sensitivity to the 'gentle whisper' (1 Kings 19:12) of the Holy Spirit guiding our prayer focus and emphasis:

Come near to God and he will come near to you.
(James 4:8)

- **Principle 12: There is no formula for prayer.** Let us articulate creative prayer in ordinary language and speak to God as we would speak to our best friend. The scriptural guide is the prayer that Jesus himself taught his disciples.

This, then, is how you should pray: 'Our Father in heaven, hallowed be your name, your kingdom come, your will be done, on earth as it is in heaven.
(Matthew 6:9-10)

- **Principle 13: Don't get distracted.** I have found that the mind can wander from the matter at hand. Also, the Christian's enemy has a strategy to bring tiredness and weariness on us like a cloud or blanket. This weight need shaking off, and praying in the Spirit (praying in tongues) helps to trigger the spiritual core within us and stimulates alertness to obstacles and lethargy. Over the years I have found the use of praise, worship and declaration of Scripture really helpful in combatting distraction.

For this reason I remind you to fan into flame the gift of God, which is in you through the laying on of my hands. For the Spirit God gave us does not make us timid, but gives us power, love and self-discipline.
(2 Timothy 1:6-7)

These are some simple, but hopefully helpful principles that will help individuals to understand and develop their prayer life and thereby benefit the prayer life of our church congregations.

2. Definitions

Throughout the guides there are a few words and phrases used that might not be familiar to some people. Here is a short list, with their definitions to help in understanding and context:

Demographic	the structure of a sector of a population
Prodigal	a person who leaves home to lead a 'prodigal' life but later makes a repentant return, as in Luke 15:11-32
Shekinah	the glory of the divine presence in Jewish and Christian theology
Five-fold gifts	a term used to describe the ministry gifts of apostle, prophet, evangelist, pastor and teacher. See Ephesians 4:11
Stand in the gap	this is a paraphrase of a scripture in Ezekiel 22:30 where God is looking for a people to intercede and watch on behalf of others
Anointing	in Scripture, the pouring of oil on a leader by a prophet symbolised the seal and calling of God to minister for him, with the expectation of the people being guided into his purposes. See Psalm 133:2
Prayer shield	the Roman shield (*Scutum*) was a large rectangular protection which aligned together in a combined (*Testudo*) formation, was at the front, behind and above. It is a great description of complete corporate prayer covering

Hedge of protection   this is a phrase that describes the protection of God that is described in Psalm 91:1: 'shelter of the Most High'; Psalm 34:7: the Lord encamping around us; Matthew 18:19: prayer of agreement in unity

Iniquity   this is a description of behaviour which is unfair and is the consequence of unacceptable or immoral actions. See Psalm 25:11 and Isaiah 53:6.

3. The Guides

I have developed these 'How to' guides in the hope that they will assist individuals, groups and churches in being more deeply informed as well as 'Engaged' in prayer. It should also help every person become more creative in personal as well as corporate prayer. Whilst they do not necessarily cover every possible topic, I sincerely want the material to be as helpful as possible in breaking new ground and building a deeper understanding of prayer as a lifestyle, thus bringing greater fruitfulness as an outcome.

The guides are in two parts:

1. An overview for *preparation*
   o The aim for the particular subject matter.
   o What is needed to be best prepared to pray effectively.
   o Engaging with the subject matter to be better informed and to understand.
   o Some practicalities relevant to the subject.
   o Some keys to help effectiveness in praying.

2. Practical *activation*, application and activities
   o A biblical perspective as a foundation.
   o Specific prayer points on the subject.
   o Practical ways to apply the prayer points and follow up.
   o A testimony of encouragement relating to the subject matter.
   o A pre-prepared prayer to actively use.
   o A helpful quote about prayer.

The list of guides can be added to. The guides are only a starting point to assist strategic prayer. There is no reason why you cannot use the same template I have designed, and build your own prayer guide. My intention is also that you could introduce your own ideas, resources and emphases in line with the situation in your community, village, town, or city.

Utilise what has been designed in this book and link it with your own research, understanding and experiences. God is amazing and there is no end to his creativity flowing through your own availability. Be blessed and encouraged as you use these guides.

There is no question that God is interested in all of our prayer, regardless of how serious, or trivial they may be. Just cry out to God in ordinary language as if Jesus was standing beside you, but treat him with the respect and honour that he deserves.
Roger Grassham

Guide 1

How to: Pray for pastors and leaders

Preparation

The aim:

The aim of this guide is to help people pray for their local and national church pastors and leaders. Our prayers are needed because pastoral ministry and leadership responsibility, although extremely rewarding, can also be a huge challenge. Praying regularly for our pastors and leaders is biblical (1 Timothy 2:2), practical and a true expression of commitment and support. It is a good thing for us to show respect for their labour, and honour for the weight of burden and responsibility they carry (1 Thessalonians 5:12-13).

What is needed:

Our pastors and leaders are in the front line in ministry as shepherds, leading people to find 'green pastures' and 'quiet waters'.[14] Everyone needs to feed on the word of God and drink of the living water of the Holy Spirit. Leaders need the rod and staff of comfort mentioned in Psalm 23:

> Even though I walk through the darkest valley, I will fear no evil, for you are with me; your rod and your staff, they comfort me.
> (Psalm 23:4)

For a church shepherd, as would be the case on a farm, the rod and staff is a means of guiding, keeping order and fighting off the enemies of the people's well-being and development. These implements are meant for correction and care respectively. Being in the vanguard of leading and caring can be a lonely place of responsibility, so we need to pray for them as if our own lives depend on it, because they do! We honour and support leaders by praying for them, so let us do it with our whole hearts. Prayer for our leaders is a command of Scripture. So, let us do it!

Engaging and understanding:
To know how to and what to pray for pastors and leaders, we need to understand the weight of the calling and responsibilities they face. Showing appreciation can be done in many ways, but here we are emphasising the need for prayer and intercession. In some churches there are designated groups of intercessors who feel called to pray regularly and consistently. So, engaging in prayer with understanding is particularly important.

> Have confidence in your leaders and submit to their authority, because they Keep watch over you as those who must give an account. Do this so that their work will be a joy, not a burden, for that would be of no benefit to you.
> (Hebrews 13:17)

The practicalities:
When praying as an individual, you seek for the Holy Spirit to lead you. If you are part of a group that has been asked to regularly pray for your pastors and leaders, then understanding the need for discretion and confidentiality is important. This builds trust and integrity between the parties and assists in the careful handling of sensitive, strategic and specific information.

Keys to effectiveness:
Some years ago I took my church ministry team and prospective leaders through an intensive leadership training programme. Part of

this training was my speaking about values that are foundational to any church, its vision and mission. These values equally apply to our preparation to pray for pastors and leaders. As an experienced pastor and leader, I know that these values apply to me too! The values are listed here to help you prepare to be effective in prayer for pastors and leaders. We should:

- seek to always walk in holiness;
- live a life of truth, integrity and honesty;
- fulfil the commands of Jesus to love and speak well of one another;
- live in intimacy with Jesus;
- worship always in 'Spirit and ... truth' (John 4:24);
- allow God room to release signs following teaching of his Word;
- be clothed in God's righteousness;
- be rooted and grounded in love and kindness;
- have compassion for the lost, broken and poor;
- read, understand, obey and apply God's Word to everyday life;
- 'pray continually' (1 Thessalonians 5:17);
- be ready for the return of Jesus Christ in the way we live.

Activation

Biblical perspective:

I urge, then, first of all, that petitions, prayers, intercession and thanksgiving be made for all people – for kings and all those in authority, that we may live peaceful and quiet lives in all godliness and holiness.
(1 Timothy 2:1-2)

Prayer points:

- For protection from the strategies of the enemy to distract, tempt and overload in work.
- For spiritual encouragement to come by the power of the Holy Spirit, overcoming stress.
- For good health and a balanced lifestyle of work, study and rest.
- For strength and enjoyment in family relationships in the home and elsewhere.
- For wisdom in leading the church and influencing the community.
- For positive team relationships of challenge and encouragement.
- For clarity and insight on vision, mission and values.
- For the ability to share the load of responsibility in delegation and teamwork.
- For good peer level fellowship, so that iron sharpens iron (Proverbs 27:17).

Application:
Find ways in which you can positively encourage people to be regular, faithful and consistent in attendance at corporate prayer meetings as well as individually and in small groups. What you pray in private sometimes needs to be declared publicly to bring encouragement and impetus to others. Be discreet in the sharing of information, to retain trust and integrity in praying for the needs shared by your pastors and leaders. Where necessary, ask for permission to share needs for prayer more widely and thereby ensure a high standard in trust and relationships. Teach, instruct and always encourage one another.

Testimony:
This is quite personal to me, but I prayerfully felt I should share it with you now:

During a three-year season of prayer and periodic times of fasting, I had a very vivid picture come into my mind. I saw the face of a man with a crown of thorns on his head, blood running down his face, but the most penetrating thing of all was his eyes. I could see the suffering, but was overwhelmed by the love. Then into my head came the words 'You will fellowship with me in suffering as you walk where I want you to go.' As you can imagine, it impacted me very deeply, more than words can say. When I look back at my life in pastoral leadership, those words and memories have brought comfort, but also a realisation that carrying the responsibilities of leadership and care for people is costly but rewarding in equal measure. There is a significant price to pay in the loneliness and faithfulness to God's calling. But equally, there is an amazing fulfilment when you see people grow and mature to fulfil their potential as disciples of Jesus. I have always said that 'whatever God calls you to, he will equip you, no matter the cost'. I have proved this to be true, and will be forever grateful to the faithful prayer warriors and intercessors who have stood in the gap for me regularly. Without their prayers I would not have been able to do it. Respect!
Roger Grassham

Prayer/Action:
Lord, help us to put into practice all that we have been taught about the importance of praying for our leaders. We want to stand 'in the gap' today for our pastors and church leadership teams. May they hear your voice speaking clearly. May your wisdom come into some

of the complicated and sensitive situations in people's lives. May there be clarity and understanding as decisions are made. We pray that your provision would be released to cover every need. Lord, you have promised to never leave us nor forsake us.[15] We pray that pastors and leaders will be conscious of your presence as they serve you and fulfil their commitments to lead, care and advise those in need. Please provide wisdom, clear direction and anointing when planning and actively doing outreach and mission. Please watch over the families of our leaders. Protect and guard their coming and going. We pray all of this in Jesus' name. Amen.

Quote:

Lord sanctify us. Oh! That Thy spirit might come and saturate every faculty, subdue every passion, and use every power of our nature for obedience to God.

Charles Spurgeon[16]

Guide 2

How to: Pray for outreach and mission

Preparation

The aim:

The aim of this guide is to help with praying for those sharing the gospel of Jesus verbally and practically through outreach into communities. Mission is God's assignment for the Church to communicate and serve both nationally and internationally. The word 'go' is often used to describe Jesus' great commission for outreach (Mark 16:15). Prayer is needed for all those who are called by God to creatively proclaim their faith in words and action. The Church 'sends out' those who fulfil this calling of bringing hope to a needy world. It is essential that they are regularly covered in prayer.

What is needed:

Evangelists, chaplains, missionaries and others are at the cutting edge of ministry to society in a variety of different ways. Much of the work is pioneering new projects, bringing specific skills, and meeting the needs of desperate people. Challenges are many and varied. Outreach and mission is necessary in places suffering from poverty, sickness, abuse, unemployment and educational lack. In such places there are personal and organisational needs. Sometimes workers are in potential danger, with divided communities and gangs operating. The need for prayer is immense, both for compassionate action and protection.

Engaging and understanding:

Those Christians who feel called to work in needy communities will make huge sacrifices and give priority to other people. Often these workers are called to a geographical area or country, specific village, town, or city. Working in struggling communities means not only giving out spiritually, but also expending a lot of time, effort and emotional energy. In some cases, the Christian message will not be welcome and will conflict with the religion of the indigenous population. In such circumstances the workers who God calls will know the risks, but still want to obey God and serve, regardless of what they may face. Other people's calling will be to affluent but godless places, which will bring its own challenges.

The practicalities:
If you know people personally, you will want to pray for them regularly. Sometimes churches have members who feel God's calling to serve him in outreach and mission. In those cases, the Church may 'send out' and support them. In other cases, people's calling is to intercede, and this is just as important. Prayer and practical support are needed on a regular basis. Whether praying for someone we know or for an organisation, there will be a concern that stimulates us to pray. Here are some keys to praying effectively.

Keys to effectiveness:
Here are some important issues people face when reaching out and on mission:

- *Motivation and purpose.* The importance of a clear call and reason for doing what is required.
- *Health.* Physical and emotional demands are significant. Responsibilities take their toll. Loneliness and isolation can be debilitating.
- *Financial support.* Financial provision may be by faith, but it still involves a lot of fundraising and research.

- *Opportunities.* Pioneering in new situations you are starting from scratch relationally.
- *Risk taking.* Activating of faith steps requires breaking new ground, which is often extremely hard.
- *Hindrances.* There are people who will oppose and create obstacles to the Christian gospel. People's attitudes may be cynical and try to create barriers to breakthrough.
- *Danger.* There is a real possibility of encountering persecution and opposition.
- *Accessibility.* Modes of transport vary, and remote places are often difficult to get to. In these cases, equipment and suitable vehicles are essential.
- *Tiredness.* There are dangers of burnout from overworking and not taking enough rest. Pioneering is hard work, and this can take its toll over time.

Activation

Biblical perspective:

He said to them, 'Go into all the world and preach the gospel to all creation.
(Mark 16:15)

Prayer points:
Here are some important things to pray for people who are reaching out and on mission:

- *Spiritual anointing* – that the call of God will be accompanied by God's giftings (1 John 2:20).
- *Physical energy* – that there will be ample stamina and strength to fulfil the needs. (Isaiah 40:28-31)

- *Financial provision* – that there will be enough financial resource for the task.
- *Open doors* – that there will be divine connections with influential people.
- *Boldness* – that faith and trust in God will bring courage and resilience in the work.
- *Effectiveness* – that the work will be fruitful and fulfilling for everyone.
- *Protection* – that wisdom and tact will be accompanied by supernatural intervention.
- *Travel* – that means of transport will be safe and secure in different locations.
- *Refreshment* – that suitable periods of rest will be found in the right venues.

Application:

The importance of praying regularly for people fulfilling a call to outreach and mission should not be underestimated. Therefore, remember to pray for individuals and teams, ideally daily, but at least weekly and on other special occasions. Create a bookmark or insert diary reminders on your phone or tablet. Have a special outreach and mission Sunday at your church. Dedicate specific church prayer meetings to remember those on the front line working in communities. Ensure that you pray discreetly and sensitively for workers who are on mission in overseas countries where knowledge of their Christian faith would put them in danger. Follow up your prayers with personal contacts to encourage and communicate your commitment to regular prayer.

Testimony:

Here are two Elim Pentecostal Church 'Elim Reach'[17] stories of life-changing encounters through outreach and mission:

A former addict of seventeen years, Trudy Makepeace was caught up in a life of crime and prostitution. In 2006 she entered a Christian Rehabilitation Centre where she met with Jesus, who radically transformed her life. She now has a passion to see people encounter God for themselves. Trudy has spoken in prisons, churches and conferences sharing her story and seeing many come to faith. She believes an encounter with God not only sets people free but gives hope, peace and purpose to their lives.

Hani Shadad was born in Sudan into a strong Muslim family and was happy living as a Muslim. His grandfather built his own mosque and was the Imam (religious leader). Hani left Sudan as a refugee in his late teens. He then married a non-Muslim and they had three children together. Hani had a powerful experience of Jesus and became a Christian believer, giving up his Muslim faith. He now travels with Elim International Missions telling others his story.

Prayer/Action:
We pray that the message of the gospel will be proclaimed worldwide through those you have called to evangelism and outreach. Lord, thank you for the sacrifice shown by those who have given up homes, jobs and wider families to serve you as missionaries overseas. We also pray for your power and anointing to be released through those who you have called to this work. Please provide, protect and energise them in Jesus' name. Amen.

Quote:

I say to you, as you pick up the mantle by faith and cross over with it,[18] the gift will make way for itself, it will be recognised, you won't have to force it or strive. God will make a way where there is no way!

Roger Grassham: a quote from the retirement message preached to River Church, Canning Town in east London July 2019

Guide 3

How to: Pray for local and national government

Preparation

The aim:

The aim of this guide is to help when praying for our elected representatives. Politicians are always a diverse group of people. Some will be Christians and will have a desire to serve their communities either as local councillors or MPs because of their firmly held beliefs for justice and deeply felt principles. The politicians will be working alongside council and government departmental staff to develop policies and exercise sound governance. Politicians and officers are in a position of responsibility and have an overwhelming need of just, wise and compassionate decision-making. Our prayers can be influential in communities spiritually and practically, and thereby have a long-term effect.

What is needed:

Our prayers and intercession are regularly needed. The apostle Paul in 1 Timothy 2:1-2 urges us to pray 'for kings and all those in authority'. Together our verbal and written communications to politicians will have an impact. We want God's love, compassion and justice to be the primary motivation as councillors and MPs carry out their responsibilities, hopefully with competence and collective agreement. We want to encourage prayer that releases stronger moral and ethical codes for life and living.

Engaging and understanding:
Often, we express our views (or opinions) about politicians. Sometimes we have our own political philosophies. However, the Scriptures do not lean towards philosophical or political bias. We are just told to pray for those in authority over us.

> Therefore, you kings, be wise; be warned, you rulers of the earth. Serve the LORD with fear and celebrate his rule with trembling. (Psalm 2:10-11)

It is vital we pray, as politicians make decisions that affect us in society. Keeping an even-handed, unbiased approach is essential, especially as people have disparate political perspectives covering every theory and ideology. This will also challenge our impartiality and attitudes.

The practicalities:
Politicians do not operate in isolation. Both councillors and MPs have support staff and advisors and MPs also have party whips to consider. Party whips are officials whose task it is to ensure party discipline by ensuring that members of the party vote according to the party platform, rather than according to their own individual ideology, or the will of their constituents. Realising that regularly there are challenging decisions to be made which are influenced by strong party-based influences will help us to pray more effectively. A politician's passion for their work might get weakened, tempered and undermined by powerful voices whose opinions might conflict with their own views. Politics is full of compromise and diplomacy. This should help us to focus our prayers for individuals and for the governing groups.

Keys to effectiveness:
Regardless of an individual's political background or ideology we need to:

- *Recognise* public servants operate from conviction and personal experience.
- *Understand* that politicians usually want to make a difference in their work.
- *Research* thoroughly, if you want your prayers to be focused and targeted effectively.
- *Build* relationships of understanding with local politicians to find out what they think.
- *Affirm* and do not criticise politicians, and try always to highlight what is done well rather than a perceived wrong.
- *Develop* factual knowledge of people, their background and their interests.
- *Listen* well to what is said in briefings and reports, in order to grasp the facts.
- *Have* consistency in prayer to establish empathy about the weight of responsibility carried.

Activation

Biblical perspective:

turning your ear to wisdom and applying your heart to understanding – indeed, if you call out for insight and cry aloud for understanding, and if you look for it as for silver and search for it as for hidden treasure, then you will understand the fear of the LORD and find the knowledge of God. For the LORD gives wisdom; from his mouth come knowledge and understanding. He holds success in store for the upright, he is a shield to those

whose way of life is blameless, for he guards the course of the just and protects the way of his faithful ones.
(Proverbs 2:2-8)

Prayer points:
The scripture most associated with prayer for political leaders is 1 Timothy 2:1-2 ('for kings and … those in authority'). The key scripture in Proverbs 2:1-8 (King Solomon's words) highlights the value of wisdom. There are important prayer points drawn from these verses. Pray for the Holy Spirit to influence politicians and their advisors, so that:

- there will be a strong desire to use wisdom and tact in decision-making processes;
- the decisions made will be based on the use of strong moral and ethical principles;
- proper attention will be paid to advice given, and that the basis of the advice will be balanced;
- there will be spiritual and intellectual insight into the formulation of policy and guidance;
- a search for hidden truth (treasure) ensures that injustice and untruth will be uncovered;
- the 'fear of the LORD' (Proverbs 1:7) grips the hearts of those governing so that God is honoured;
- knowledge and understanding will guide the governance of our councils and Parliament;
- integrity will be evident in lifestyle and in everything that is decided;
- scrutiny of process and decisions brings justice and the setting of accountability structures.

Application:
Councillors, MPs and their advisors are responsible for governance of a wide range of areas. These will include Health, Education, Social Care, Housing, Benefits, Public Highway, Leisure, Police, Planning, Business and many other areas where licensing and registration is necessary. When you pray, try to focus on one or more of the above areas; get to know the elected officials by name and be aware of how decisions made have an impact in your community. Why not let them know you are praying for them.

Testimony:
There are testimonies of how MPs got involved in politics and the difference that their faith makes to their work in Parliament. You can access and hear the stories here: www.christiansinparliament.org.uk/about/members-stories/.[19]
It is amazing to hear how each of the MPs have come to faith and understanding of Christian values in different ways. Typically these include: being born into a home with Christian values; finding God at university whilst studying; engaging in community outreach work and seeing the huge influence people of faith have amongst the needy and disadvantaged in society. In every case God moved in a different way, but everyone carries the Christian values with them and tries to apply them in the work they do in their constituencies, and in Parliament overall.

Prayer/Action:
Father God, we pray for our politicians. Lord, our nation needs leaders both nationally and locally with discerning hearts and wise minds. We come to you today, asking you to give us wise leaders that will lead in the right direction. We pray that no corruption will creep into their life and work and that they live in accordance with

your Word. Let our politicians and their advisors be people who honour your holy Name, for it is only from you that they will get true wisdom. Give our politicians insight and humility, that they may be able to do things beyond their understanding. Help them to choose the right path when they make decisions on behalf all of us. We ask this in the mighty name of Jesus. Amen.

Quote:

Our prayer must not be self-centered. It must arise not only because we feel our own need as a burden we must lay upon God, but also because we are so bound up in love for our fellow men that we feel their need as acutely as our own. To make intercession for men is the most powerful and practical way in which we can express our love for them.[20]
John Calvin

Guide 4

How to: Pray for Parliament

Preparation

The aim:
The aim of this guide is to help in praying for Members of Parliament (MPs). Regardless of our individual political views, we need to pray for all MPs collectively – they are responsible for decisions affecting the whole country.

Who are they?
Stated simply, Parliament is a legislature that functions as a body of people with the institutional power to discuss and decide on matters of state. MPs are members who represent people from their constituency.

What do they do?
A parliament has three functions, i.e. representation, legislation and parliamentary control. This is when enquiries, hearings, committees and debates are organised on laws, and processes are scrutinised. An MP is someone who people have elected to represent them in a Parliament. The whole group have power to introduce laws, change them and generally govern the whole country.

What is needed:
In the UK, MPs are democratically elected and represent their constituencies in Parliament. There are many pressures that MPs face, and they are called upon to make immense decisions individually (by voting in Parliament) and together (sometimes lobbied on party lines). Be aware that the 'Party Whip' is a person

who ensures party discipline is upheld, especially when there is a need to vote as a collective group. The dilemma for MPs is often the balance of decisions which can sometimes clash with strongly held views, personal beliefs, moral and ethical principles. Not all UK politicians are Christians, although a number are. However, the Scriptures do not differentiate when it comes to prayer for leaders. In accordance with Scripture, our responsibility is to pray for all in authority over us.

> I urge, then, first of all, that petitions, prayers, intercession and thanksgiving be made for all people – for kings and all those in authority, that we may live peaceful and quiet lives in all godliness and holiness.
> (1 Timothy 2:1-2)

Engaging and understanding:
There are four main themes given in 1 Timothy 2:1. These help us understand how to engage in prayer for our MPs and Parliament as a whole:

a) *Petitions* are *a humble and sincere appeal to someone who has the power to grant a request.* What should be our petition for MPs? Pray that they will have wisdom, understanding and godly standards. All need the 'fear of the LORD (Proverbs 1:7)'; wisdom comes as a result.

b) *Prayers* are *the act or practise of a spoken or unspoken address to God,* constantly and consistently for MPs and their families.

c) *Intercession* is pleading on somebody's behalf, which means we are to be an advocate, by 'standing in the gap'.

d) *Thanksgiving* is an expression or act of giving thanks. It may also be public acknowledgement or celebration of God's divine goodness.

The practicalities:
When you pray, consider how MPs need: discretion, humility, teachability, diligence, decisiveness and right standing with everyone.

Keys to effectiveness:

- *Good character.* Integrity and being well thought of by people for the right reasons.
- *Moral standing.* The ability to treat everyone as equals and with respect, and as individuals they lead by example.
- *Advocacy.* Having the skills to represent others and the ability to support and find answers for their need, without prejudice.
- *Balance.* Needed in lifestyle, work and family, so the MP is able to be as effective as possible in the role. (MPs spend a lot of time away from home while in Parliament.)
- *Belief...* in the work they do, and the right motivation for doing it!

Activation
Biblical perspective:

Let everyone be subject to the governing authorities, for there is no authority except that which God has established. The authorities that exist have been established by God.
(Romans 13:1)

Prayer points:

- For ability to think clearly in an unbiased way that honours the people being represented.
- For care and understanding in matters that affect lives, remembering that it is all about people.
- For wisdom and understanding in dealing with complex matters.
- For inspirational leadership.

Do not be afraid; you will not be put to shame. Do not fear disgrace; you will not be humiliated. You will forget the shame of your youth and remember no more the reproach of your widowhood.
(Isaiah 54:4)

- For good health.

Dear friend, I pray that you may enjoy good health and that all may go well with you, just as you are progressing spiritually.
(3 John 1:2)

- For protection for home and possessions when travelling, and to guard against unnecessary intrusions on time. Also, to guard against temptations in relationships while being away from home.

Application:

There are some very practical things that you can do:

- Find out who your local MP is and pray for them by name, for their family and safety.
- Find out whether they have a governmental role as a minister, and in what department.
- Pray for all the advisors and administrators that support your MP.
- Pray for balance in time and influence in constituency and national government issues.
- Write to your MP to let them know that you and your church are praying for them.
- Ask your MP what you can pray for them about.
- Thank your MP for the time they give and for their service. Encourage and bless them.
- Never forget the spiritual dimension. Powerful influences operate and affect our MPs.

Testimony:

I was brought up to believe that my good start in life meant that I owed a debt to others less fortunate and this gained a new perspective with my growing faith. As a hereditary Peer elected to an – as yet – life Peerage (in itself a privilege), it looks as if that will remain the template of my life till it ends. If only I could fill it! I also exercise, to the best of my ability, a small ministry of prayer for those Parliamentarians I, and some of my friends, known to be specially in need of it.

Lord Rodney Elton[21]

Prayer/Action:

Lord, we are really concerned about the society in which we live. Our MPs have some influence locally and vote on matters of national importance. Please guide and bring wisdom to my local MP and help them to make righteous decisions that will affect all of us. Please cover and protect our MPs and keep them from harm as they go about their important business in our country's capital city. We pray that policy advisors and influencers around our MPs will only suggest statements and actions that are righteous and true. Help us to pray for our MPs when there are local and national emergencies. We also pray for honesty and transparency in matters affecting our lives. Please also protect our MPs from unhelpful distractions that might divert them away from their primary purpose. Lord, we give you thanks for our MPs and ask you for inspiration and understanding about ways that we, the Church, can support and affirm our elected representatives in practical ways. Amen.

Quote:

To be a Christian without prayer is no more possible than to be alive without breathing.
Martin Luther[22]

Guide 5

How to: Pray for your community

Preparation

The aim:

The aim of this guide is to help in praying for your local community. Your area will differ from others, and will include a diversity of settlements, types and sizes.

What is needed:

What is 'Community'? It means a group of people who are gathered together for common interest and support, who may also be living in the same area, and who are also affected by everything that happens around them. This guide focuses on your geographical area and the people living nearby. You may live in a village, town, or city. Regardless, communities are about people. So, focus on your neighbours, street, gathering places, where footfall is greatest and where conversations and collective activity enables people to bond and form a support network.

Engaging and understanding:

Communities are based on relationships, common interests and sharing. Views vary on how best to establish a cohesive 'place' for people to be together. Living near each other inevitably brings some tensions and pressure, simply because it is difficult to get agreements. Architects and town planners often refer to 'place making' when regenerating rundown areas. Fundamentally, people working together is essential and must be a conscious decision. The need for diplomacy and consensus is paramount. Those of us who are part of a local church will have experienced just how hard it is to get agreement on decisions affecting everyone. How much more difficult it is in a locality for people of diverse backgrounds, and whose motives are quite different and not based on Christian principles, to work in harmony. It is for us to find ways to engage in community and gain mutual respect and understanding. The local church can bring a positive influence, thus encouraging harmony and cohesion. This scripture applies to the Church but can equally relate to the wider community:

> I appeal to you, brothers and sisters, in the name of our Lord Jesus Christ, that all of you agree with one another in what you say and that there be no divisions among you, but that you be perfectly united in mind and thought.
> (1 Corinthians 1:10)

The practicalities:
Our communities will be affected by a wide range of influences, both local and national. The sort of areas that we should be aware of include:

- children and families, for education and leisure;
- common economic influences, such as retail shops, services, and businesses;
- safety, security and vulnerability, which are a concern for the elderly and small children;
- influential groups that make decisions affecting the environment and amenities;
- demographics of home ownership, affordable accommodation for homeless people, and attitudes to each group;

- established Church influence. In any community, the presence of other faith groups need consideration;
- ethnic diversity, family dynamics and value systems;
- festivals that happen regularly as part of local tradition and customs imported from other cultures.

Keys to effectiveness:
The cohesion within local communities is largely relational, and therefore influenced by:

- *kindness* as a choice when communicating with one another;
- *love* as an underlying attitude that enables all people to relate to one another;
- *care* for one another by being attentive to the diverse needs among people of all ages;
- *organising* activities that are for the benefit of everyone, with no exception;
- *creating* a relaxed atmosphere by having fun, and celebrating milestones;
- *being courteous* in tackling difficulties that arise from time to time;
- *wisdom* when resolving conflicts between divided people and groups;
- *sensitivity* about behaviour and traditions.

Activation

Biblical perspective:

Carry each other's burdens, and in this way you will fulfil the law of Christ.
(Galatians 6:2)

And we urge you, brothers and sisters, warn those who are idle and disruptive, encourage the disheartened, help the weak, be patient with everyone.
(1 Thessalonians 5:14)

May the God who gives endurance and encouragement give you the same attitude of mind toward each other that Christ Jesus had, so that with one mind and one voice you may glorify the God and Father of our Lord Jesus Christ.
(Romans 15:5-6)

Prayer points:
How and what do we pray, then? The scriptures above help bring some focus; for example, sharing burdens, supporting the needy and bringing encouragement. Because we also influence by our actions, we pray for:

- a heart of compassion for those who are most vulnerable in our community (Matthew 9:36);
- opportunities to influence community leaders and give them support and encouragement;
- our doctors, nurses and medical staff, for wisdom, alertness and their own health;
- our police and community support officers, for their safety and for impartiality in what they do;
- our emergency services' teams as they respond to health and well-being events;
- our council workers and amenity staff as they keep essential services and utilities running;
- our schools and colleges' expertise and care as they educate our children and students (Proverbs 22:6);

- charities, their volunteers, funding and resources so they are effective in delivering care/support;
- the staff running general stores, post offices and other essential service outlets;
- those working in industry, commerce, banking and retail, as they provide goods and services for the diverse needs in society.

Application:

While churches themselves offer opportunity for spiritual well-being, there are public benefit services provided by them too. As you pray for the areas mentioned above, consider engaging in, and praying about:

- becoming an elected or co-opted councillor in your local parish or borough/council;
- becoming a volunteer in local charities to bring Christian love and influence;
- being a visitor to local care homes or hospices;
- offering to shop for a vulnerable person living nearby, or maybe doing their garden;
- getting training to be a classroom assistant in a local school, to assist with helping pupils learn to read and/or supporting the teacher.

You may already be engaged in community service and pray before, during and after serving. Your church, home group or prayer team can support you through prayer. There are many people serving as chaplains and in other areas of community service. Commit to pray for them regularly by name.

Testimony:
This is an extract from the Elim Pentecostal Churches Annual Report 2018:[23]

I once sat listening to a woman on a cancer ward who was scared to leave her 15-year-old daughter. I came off the ward and cried and told God that I couldn't do it anymore. He said, 'No you can't do it, but I can.' That's when I realised I wasn't doing this in my own strength. A chaplain is someone who carries the presence of God, bringing peace and comfort, and a calmness in the midst of panic. It's not wrong to prepare people for death or pray for healing, but you should do it in a tender, sensitive way. *Ann Stevenson, former lead chaplain at Sandwell and West Birmingham hospitals NHS Trust*

Prayer/Action:
Dear Lord, we ask you to use us, and the Church as a whole in reaching our community. Help us to be ambassadors for your kingdom by practical service and in the giving of time, skills and compassion in Jesus' name. Amen.

Quote:

The exclusion of the weak and insignificant, the seemingly useless people, from a Christian community may actually mean the exclusion of Christ; in the poor brother Christ is knocking at the door.
Dietrich Bonhoeffer[24]

Guide 6

How to: Pray for children and young people

Preparation

The aim:

The aim of this guide is to help in praying for children and youth of all ages and backgrounds. This includes a desire to see God's strength and influence in their learning and development, so that they fulfil their potential, enjoy life, and deal with peer pressure. Also, to see the development of wisdom in their lifestyle, and the ability to endure through hardship, shocks and emergencies.

What is needed:

Our children and the young people are a blessing from the Lord. Their growth and development will be shaped by their families, friendships, educational establishments and the things that they see, hear and do. With so many different voices, we need to pray that they are taught by good examples; that their lives are shaped by positive influences, and that they are able to discern negative voices that will try to lead them astray. We need to understand the power of the media, games, peer pressure and other forces that are at work outside of the safety of family. Some of the national institutional policies and teachings may conflict with biblical teachings. Prayer will help cover the children and the young people as they learn to recognise and handle information that may differ with Christian discipleship teaching and lifestyle.

Engaging and understanding:
There are so many potential influences on our children and young people, and so our prayers need to be targeted on some specific areas which will include:

a) home and family environment;
b) friendships;
c) school and college;
d) sports and recreation;
e) peer pressures and controlling influences;
f) the internet, games and social media;
g) sexuality and development in social interaction;
h) adolescence;
i) behaviour;
j) mental and emotional health;
k) advertising.

It is essential that our prayers are informed. Children and young people are inherently relational, and their desire for community, family and individual identity within groups is a high priority.

Wisdom and tact are essential in handling this area due to the heightened sensitivities in society in general. Awareness of policies and procedures regarding safeguarding are needed where information and personal details are requested. Approaching this subject sensitively and wisely will help avoid misunderstandings. Bear in mind some children and young people will have disabilities or emotional disorders, and these require sensitive handling. Some may be fostered or adopted, so requiring a safe and stable environment to develop positively.

The practicalities:
As part of children's and young people's growth, they will learn and develop understanding from a range of areas. Today, much of this will be from what they read, see others doing and by investigation and experimentation. Parents and guardians will not always be aware what children and young people are doing, so prayer is essential for covering, protection and the guidance and influence of the Holy Spirit.

Keys to effectiveness:
The keys to effectiveness in praying for children and young people will include having:

- *consistency* and regularity in our approach;
- *dependability* and respect in our attitudes;
- *genuine love* for the well-being and best interests of children and young people;
- *compassion* for the life challenges faced every day;
- *sympathy* for those who have experienced trauma and/or life-limiting disorders (for example, autism, ADHD etc.);
- *sensitivity* and care for those in poverty, in debt, or who are in care;
- *awareness* of those children and young people that need a new sense of safety and a place of refuge;
- *understanding* about the uncertainty, injustice and vulnerability that young people can feel day to day;
- *recognition* of the need for children and young people to 'belong' in a healthy, supportive family atmosphere.

Activation

Biblical perspective:

Children are a heritage from the LORD, offspring a reward from him.
(Psalm 127:3)

Start children off on the way they should go, and even when they are old they will not turn from it.
(Proverbs 22:6)

Don't let anyone look down on you because you are young, but set an example for the believers in speech, in conduct, in love, in faith and in purity.
(1 Timothy 4:12)

Prayer points:
There are some key matters to focus on in prayer for children and young people.

Children
- As children grow, we pray that they will develop in general well-being and maturity.
- We pray that they will have a stable and loving family environment that will be stimulating and bring joy.
- May new babies, toddlers and older children stay healthy and be free of allergies and generational illnesses.
- May they have positive experiences as they learn to interact and play with other children.
- Pray that their growth mentally, emotionally and intellectually will be appropriate for their age.

- May their homes and community be places of safety and security.
- May their homes and family be or become God-fearing and God-honouring.

Young people
- May the young people develop friendships and relationships that maintain respect for people and the law.
- Pray for a protective guard around them in the use of the internet, and especially the use of social media.
- May they have awareness that their personal identity is made 'in the image of God' (Genesis 1:27).
- May they learn to make lifestyle choices that find ways of steering clear of addictive substances and activity.
- May God guide them that they may learn to have a healthy respect for parents, guardians and those in authority.
- Pray that every young person finds Jesus as Lord and Saviour, and good fellowship within a local church.
- Pray that they will seek to develop their God-given potential with further education and to maximise available opportunities.
- Pray that they develop compassionate, generous hearts to serve, including during gap year and volunteering.

Application:
Prayer for children and young people may then honour those looking after them, by finding ways to affirm their parents' or guardians' sacrificial giving to their children. The bi-product will be a strong bond between whole families and the church. Remember, there is a 'Limitless'[25] wealth of potential and creativity that may be untapped in children and the youth.

Encourage children to pray and participate corporately. Encourage the young people by providing opportunities to contribute and input into church life and activity. Create an atmosphere that nurtures, mentors and provides opportunities for the youth.

Pioneer new ideas and be prepared to experiment by encouraging the young people to express their creativity, zeal and freshness in approach. Inclusivity will bring a strong and affirming family feel.

Testimony:

On the Elim Pentecostal Church – Limitless Kids website,[26] Nadia Bashir shares on the importance of praying for the kids who come into our care, about us being watchmen and watchwomen, not just physically but also spiritually.

Limitless Oxygen, a training event designed for youth workers and held annually,[27] records the following testimony: 'the creation of a valuable space for us to receive from God, get practical input, great ideas and seminars to help us be equipped to serve our young people better. I came away feeling encouraged, renewed and stirred to keep investing in the next generation' said by Annie Skett, former youth pastor of Encounter Church, Selly Oak (2013-2017).

Prayer/Action:

Dear Lord, help us to be encouragers of children and young people. Use us to create a safe and secure environment for children and youth so that they are given the maximum opportunity to grow and fulfil their potential. Give us a deep desire to faithfully watch and pray for them regularly. Amen.

Quote:

The best thing to spend on your children is your time.
Louise Hart[28]

Guide 7

How to: Pray for church plants and evangelism

Preparation

The aim:

The aim of this guide is to help in praying for the people and teams pioneering church plants and evangelism. These thoughts should aid prayer cover for individuals and groups that are launching initiatives in districts where a church wants to pioneer into new areas and expand its outreach. Outreach into the area may be for the first time, or reawaken a historic move of God in estates, villages, towns and cities across the country.

What is needed:

Churches want to see God's kingdom and the power of God released across our nation. Gods 'workers' will be people who have a passion for lost souls and have a calling to evangelise and/or plant new churches in areas that have been identified as ready to sow, cultivate and reap. Individuals, families and teams need preparing, training and equipping for the task. Sometimes preparation will take years, until the ground is prepared, the timing is right and the people are ready. Five-fold ministry giftings will be utilised to reach out and release the salvation message with 'signs following' (Mark 16:20, KJV). Resources are required, plans need preparing and refining, and support structures should be put in place. More than anything, spiritual preparation will have been undertaken, accompanied by prayer, fasting and intercession over an extended period. Some new plants may have already begun, so prayer to sustain, strengthen and protect everyone involved will be needed.

Engaging and understanding:
The calling of God will be received to evangelise and plant out. The kind of emphasis will vary depending on the geographical and demographic location, and will depend on the specific people groups that need to be reached. It is usual for 'spiritual mapping' to take place in advance. This will include researching the geographical area, looking at social needs, finding out the greatest influences on people's lifestyle and behaviour patterns, and especially profiling the needs that require the greatest support and loving input. Knowing the primary vision is essential, as is ensuring that the core gospel message is at the heart of everything that is planned and delivered. Often, the demographical make-up of a population and the significant controlling forces pervading that society will be linked to spiritual influences that are dominant and evident. Fundamentally, those called to plant will often be prepared to give sacrificially and will carry a burden for the welfare of an area they know, and that needs spiritual transformation (Jeremiah 29:7).

The practicalities:
Evangelism and church planting require investment in commitment, time, resources and finance. It is essential to have God's prophetic guidance to ensure reaching out to the right place with the right people at the right time. Energy, creativity and innovation will be hallmarks of a pioneering work of God. There is no system or formula that can be copied, but there are biblical and experiential principles, values and giftings that come together. When combined with God's anointing upon the people, amazing fruit and growth can be expected. There are some fundamental principles that are keys for effectiveness when strategy planning.

Keys to effectiveness:

- *Clear vision* will give clarity on the people groups most in need.
- *Targeted prayer* will empower every facet of the proposed evangelism and church planting.
- *Conversations* with influential and knowledgeable people within local communities will give understanding.
- *Ask* people for help and resources to support the outreach.
- *Timing* is of the essence when it comes to launching a pioneering work.
- *Risk-taking* will always be part of a pioneering initiative.
- *Unity* and shared objectives will produce the most fruit.
- *Understanding* the likely hardships is important, as well as expecting good results.
- *Researching* the new area thoroughly will help to avoid obstacles and barriers to effectiveness.

Activation

Biblical perspective:

Then Jesus came to them and said, 'All authority in heaven and on earth has been given to me. Therefore go and make disciples of all nations, baptising them in the name of the Father and of the Son and of the Holy Spirit, and teaching them to obey everything I have commanded you. And surely I am with you always, to the very end of the age.'
(Matthew 28:18-20)

But many who heard the message believed; so the number of men who believed grew to about five thousand.
(Acts 4:4)

Now in the church at Antioch there were prophets and teachers: Barnabas, Simeon called Niger, Lucius of Cyrene, Manaen (who had been brought up with Herod the tetrarch) and Saul. While they were worshipping the Lord and fasting, the Holy Spirit said, 'Set apart for me Barnabas and Saul for the work to which I have called them.' So after they had fasted and prayed, they placed their hands on them and sent them off.
(Acts 13:1-3)

Prayer points:
In the gospel scripture above, we read of Jesus commissioning the disciples, and in Acts we read of the Spirit-filled apostles' preaching, teaching and their seeing the supernatural demonstration of God's power – but they also faced opposition. Constant prayer is essential to see pioneering evangelism and church planting established.

- Pray that people will come to faith when they hear the gospel message boldly declared.
- Pray that people will recognise the source of practical love and see the good works as God's love in action.
- Pray that people will be supernaturally healed and set free by the power of the Holy Spirit.
- Pray that people in the middle of relationship breakdowns and turmoil will find hope and restoration.
- Pray that the evangelism teams and church planters will have boldness and faith as they fulfil God's call.
- Pray that the teams sent out to pioneer will experience God's anointing and fruitfulness in ministry.
- Pray that small groups of people hungry to know more will be taught and established in Bible truths.

- Pray that outreach will be effective and become known as a positive addition within the local community.
- Pray that outreach team members remain healthy and strong and will experience the strength of the Lord.

Application:
When praying for pioneering teams, constant encouragement is needed. Personal contact and the demonstration of practical love towards them will be significant in sustaining and maintaining energy, zeal and effectiveness. The demanding work saps energy. There may be little obvious return in the early stages; however, consistently and faithfully sowing and nurturing reaps a harvest and 'fruit that will last' (John 15:16).

Testimony:

I had the enormous privilege of planting a new church in Canning Town in Newham in east London. Our church had a growing congregation in need of space. God knew, as I was soon approached by another local church to consider working together. They had a huge suite of buildings and a congregation in need of support and re-envisioning. Working collaboratively with both leadership teams and congregations, together with the united churches in the borough, we set about praying and seeking God for spiritual and practical confirmations. Together we felt God say 'merge together and create a new church' when spending time in prayer and fasting. Prophetic words[29] of confirmation came, and River Church was birthed in September 2003. Looking back, I realise God had initiated a fundamental change of direction. Instead of just in-reach, he realigned us into emphasising outreach, from just being a safe family church into an army of people whose primary new direction was mission to the community. This could not have happened without extensive times of prayer and prophetic foundations. I am so grateful to God for the faithfulness of my associate pastor and team for daring to believe God on the risky but fulfilling journey. Seventeen years on, the church and community centre continue to flourish. God answers prayer.

Roger Grassham

Prayer/Action:

Lord Jesus, we pray for our evangelists and church-planting teams, that they would always be envisioned by you and stay close to you. I pray they will always be filled with the power of the Holy Spirit and draw their strength and energy from him. I pray that the teams would experience unity, boldness, endurance and protection. Keep each person in good health, equipped, resourced and in harmony with their teams. May your purposes be fulfilled in the place and with the people with whom you have called them to work. In Jesus' name. Amen.

Quote:

God takes failures and uses them for His glory. The more inadequate you feel the more you are qualified in God's eyes. That is where faith and obedience to God comes in as we break through barriers of fear and self-consciousness.

Roger Grassham[30]

Guide 8

How to: Pray and engage in spiritual warfare

Preparation

The aim:
The aim of this guide is to help in understanding the spiritual battle we have as Christians, which feels like warfare. Also, how to engage in it as part of an individual's prayer life, and corporately as part of the church prayer strategy.

What is needed:
Prayer is something that brings about change and creates space for God to move. Prayer is communication with God, and he hears and responds to our intercessions. Our problem is that the devil hates us doing this and will try to find ways to hinder and stop this happening, often affecting circumstances. It is essential to be alert to this and prepare our hearts and minds, with determination not to be distracted. If we position ourselves ready and dressed in the 'full armour of God' (Ephesians 6:10-20), possibilities for breakthrough emerge, and in faith, we pray prayers that get answered.

Engaging and understanding:
There are some basic processes fundamental to effective prayers in a spiritual battle. These include:

- *Fast* to focus the mind and body and deal with the challenges of human nature.
- *Read Scripture* to ensure sound doctrine and theology, just as Jesus did as he faced the temptations of Satan after his water baptism. See Matthew 4:1-11.

- *Pray in the Spirit*, use the gift of tongues[31] to intercede, to bring God's presence if words fail you.
- *Speak the name of Jesus.* There is power in his name.
- *Posture helps.* Stand, kneel, or lie prostrate. It helps us to submit to God and is purposeful.
- *Worship.* Declare Scripture. Sing songs of declaration and intimacy. It brings his presence. See Joshua 6:4-5. Rams' horns were used as instruments of warfare.
- *Understanding* that challenges often precede prayer. Embrace these and break through.
- *Recognise distractions* and stay focused.
- *Listen to God speaking through each other* and be sensitive to themes that emerge. This might include someone sharing a mental picture or quoting a specific scripture.
- *Touch heaven.* See tangible changes both physically and spiritually. *Take authority* over the powers of darkness and declare the power in the blood of Jesus. See Luke 10:19.
- *Use the gifts of the Spirit.*[32] Discern the spirits, pray and dispel evil influence accordingly. *Remember your authority* is in Christ. See Luke 9:1.

The practicalities:
Battle in prayer should be focused and purposeful to the circumstance. Always be strategic in warfare prayer, but sensitive and responsive. Practise brings experience and awareness.

Keys to effectiveness:

- Be filled with the Holy Spirit daily, hourly. How? Pause, confess your need to be filled with Gods power, ask God to fill you afresh, then receive and say thank you afterwards. Also, encourage one another in practical ways. 'Instead, be filled with the Spirit, speaking to one another with psalms, hymns, and songs from the Spirit. Sing and make music from your heart to the Lord' (Ephesians 5:18-19).

- Praise and worship are a significant factor in achieving breakthrough (Judges 7:15-20). Trumpets, jars and torches used to defeat the enemies of God's people.
- Let God speak through circumstances, dreams, visions, scripture and other means. Remember all authority should be under authority. Always be servant-hearted. Even Jesus knew he was under authority (John 5:19).
- When addressing 'rulers' and 'powers' (Ephesians 6:12) in the demonic realm, remember people's humanity. Exercise pastoral care with people, as well as address the spiritual realm.
- Humility in attitude as well as purposefulness in spirit is a good combination.
- Ensure you keep a short account with God on your own lifestyle as you pray and minister.

Activation

Biblical perspective:

Finally, be strong in the Lord and in his mighty power. Put on the full armour of God, so that you can take your stand against the devil's schemes. For our struggle is not against flesh and blood, but against the rulers, against the authorities, against the powers of this dark world and against the spiritual forces of evil in the heavenly realms. Therefore put on the full armour of God, so that when the day of evil comes, you may be able to stand your ground, and after you have done everything, to stand. Stand firm then, with the belt of truth buckled round your

waist, with the breastplate of righteousness in place, and with your feet fitted with the readiness that comes from the gospel of peace. In addition to all this, take up the shield of faith, with which you can extinguish all the flaming arrows of the evil one. Take the helmet of salvation and the sword of the Spirit, which is the word of God.
(Ephesians 6:10-17)

Prayer points:
Let us pray that

- every person would prepare themselves for battle by keeping a short account with God and walking in holiness, truth and integrity;
- every Christian ensures that they are a part of and accountable to an established local expression of Church authority;
- a prayer shield be established covering front line ministry, evangelism, church planting, children's and youth work, industry, commerce, health and governance, etc.;
- the Church would have good relations with local government, neighbours and influencers in your village, town or city;
- crime would reduce, and perpetrators be caught;
- God's people who have responsibilities in the community would be protected and God's kingdom advanced;
- a 'hedge of protection' would be around all the social action, education and practical outreach of the Church in the community, especially with children and young people.

Application:
Think carefully about the challenges people face every day. Face down the demands to compromise ethically and morally. Resist

temptation to compromise, cover up truth and undermine integrity. Uphold standards. Be compassionate where some may be abusive and misunderstand easily. Make a stand in the workplace. Ask for wisdom in the workplace in the face of an erosion-of biblical principles and Christian ethics.

Testimony:

On my way home from work and due to attend a church leaders' meeting, I rode my motorbike on a slippery road surface, wet from a downpour of rain. Suddenly, the front wheel began to slide as I hit an oil patch. I began to lose control of the bike. Instinctively I cried out 'Jesus!' through my helmet's facemask. Immediately the bike rectified its upright position. During the homeward journey I thanked God for his protection, supernatural intervention, and angelic assistance.
Roger Grassham

Prayer/Action:

Lord, as we face the day today, we choose to dress ourselves in the spiritual armour you have provided. Help us to stay alert and be attuned to the gifts and leadings of the Holy Spirit. May we discern and be aware of your presence and be alert to the enemy's distractions. We affirm the complete work of sacrifice of the cross and the victory that Jesus won as we affirm his resurrection through the empty tomb. Amen.

Quote:

Before a man can bind the enemy, he must know there is nothing binding him.
Smith Wigglesworth[33]

Guide 9

How to: Pray for the baptism in the Holy Spirit and gifts

Preparation

The aim:

The aim of this guide is to outline the basic understanding required to pray for people to be baptised in the Holy Spirit and to be released in the gifts of the Holy Spirit. The premise is that God wants everyone to be filled with the Holy Spirit and to flow in his gifts. Prayer may be for an individual or a group.

What is needed:

There are foundational elements to consider when praying for someone to be filled with the Holy Spirit. Importantly, they apply to both the person praying and the person being prayed for.

a) The person should already be born again or, if they are willing, to repent, believe, and accept Jesus as Lord and Saviour. Also, the person needs to be willing to step out in faith to receive all that God gives. Baptism simply means 'to be immersed in'!

b) The person recognises the need to be empowered to witness and desires all that God has made available in accordance with a Pentecostal understanding.

c) The person is ready to receive prayer and recognises that the gifts of the Holy Spirit are given and released by the Holy Spirit himself (the Giver) as part of the impartation from God.

d) A deep desire for God's presence, and recognition of the need to be totally dependent on him.

Engaging and understanding:
The baptism of the Holy Spirit was first experienced by the disciples in the upper room at Pentecost. The Holy Spirit was sent by Jesus to release the power to witness with 'signs following' (Mark 16:20, KJV). It was the promise throughout Scripture and can be seen in both the Old Testament (in Joel 2:28: 'And afterwards, I will pour out my Spirit on all people. Your sons and daughters will prophesy, your old men will dream dreams, your young men will see visions' – 'the promise') and in the New (in Acts 2:17: 'In the last days, God says, I will pour out my Spirit on all people. Your sons and daughters will prophesy, your young men will see visions, your old men will dream dreams'; see also Acts 2:4 – 'the fulfilment of promise'). Praying for someone to be baptised in the Holy Spirit may include the laying on of hands, but not always.

God's supernatural impartation has four key purposes. The work of the Holy Spirit is to fulfil God's purposes in us. Always remember these things:

1. He is the 'Helper' (*Comforter* or *Parakletos* in Greek) to lead us into all *truth* and is the 'Spirit of truth'. 'And I will ask the Father, and he will give you another advocate to help you and be with you for ever— the Spirit of truth. The world cannot accept him, because it neither sees him nor knows him. But you know him, for he lives with you and will be in you' (John 14:16-17).

2. He is the 'Power' of God (*Dunamis* in Greek) that comes upon us. 'But you will receive power when the Holy Spirit comes on you; and you will be my witnesses in Jerusalem, and in all Judea and Samaria, and to the ends of the earth' (Acts 1:8).

3. He always points towards and brings glory to Jesus. 'I have much more to say to you, more than you can now bear. But

when he, the Spirit of truth, comes, he will guide you into all the truth. He will not speak on his own; he will speak only what he hears, and he will tell you what is yet to come. He will glorify me because it is from me that he will receive what he will make known to you' (John 16:12-14).

4. The gifts of the Spirit are for the edification of the Church (the common good). 'Now to each one the manifestation of the Spirit is given for the common good' (1 Corinthians 12:7).

The practicalities:
Every individual is important to God. A personal approach is helpful, but prayer for a group is equally effective.

There is no formula or special method on how to pray. The Holy Spirit himself will lead you. Those praying for someone will need to be disciples of Jesus who have knowledge of God and are filled with the Holy Spirit. In some instances, people can get born again and filled with the Holy Spirit all at the same time. I repeat, there is no formula, and the Holy Spirit will move independently of us, as he wills.

Keys to effectiveness:

- Make sure you have a desire for the person to be blessed and used by God.
- Make sure you are fully yielded to God, to his will and to his ways.
- Understand it is the 'prayer offered in faith' (James 5:15) God uses, and believe that God will answer.
- Establish trust and relationship with the person you are praying for.
- Affirm and inspire the person you are praying for, and be sure of their spiritual progress.

- Ask whether they have ever seen anyone prayed for and filled with the Holy Spirit. Use scripture to establish the need, and explain that this is something that God wants for them. For example, some people are not aware of the work of the Holy Spirit: 'While Apollos was at Corinth, Paul took the road through the interior and arrived at Ephesus. There he found some disciples and asked them, "Did you receive the Holy Spirit when you believed?" They answered, "No, we have not even heard that there is a Holy Spirit"' (Acts 19:1-2).
- Explain that the gifts of the Holy Spirit are part of the package when baptised in the Holy Spirit.
- Help people to concentrate on the 'Giver' and not on the 'gifts'. Follow-up teaching will help here.

Activation

Biblical perspective:

Prophecy
'Follow the way of love and eagerly desire gifts of the Spirit, especially prophecy... Two or three prophets should speak, and the others should weigh carefully what is said.'
(1 Corinthians 14:1,29)

Promise
'And I will ask the Father, and he will give you another advocate to help you and be with you for ever – the Spirit of truth. The world cannot accept him, because it neither sees him nor knows him. But you know him, for he lives with you and will be in you.'
(John 14:16-17)

Practice

When the day of Pentecost came, they were all together in one place. Suddenly a sound like the blowing of a violent wind came from heaven and filled the whole house where they were sitting. They saw what seemed to be tongues of fire that separated and came to rest on each of them. All of them were filled with the Holy Spirit and began to speak in other tongues as the Spirit enabled them.

(Acts 2:1-4)

Edification

Now to each one the manifestation of the Spirit is given for the common good. To one there is given through the Spirit a message of wisdom, to another a message of knowledge by means of the same Spirit … All these are the work of one and the same Spirit, and he distributes them to each one, just as he determines.

(1 Corinthians 12:7-11)

Prayer points:

Now let us pray in faith for God to touch the person, or people.

Baptism of the Holy Spirit

- Release his power upon and within the person and remove any self-consciousness, inhibitions, or obstacles.
- Reassure them that they are loved and someone God wants to empower and use.
- Enable them to abandon themselves to the Lord that he may increase within them.
- Experience the power, presence and peace of the Holy Spirit as they wait upon God to receive.

- Have a deep desire for more of God's fullness in their lives and for them to surrender fully to his purposes.
- Have an increased level of faith in God's promises.

Gifts of the Holy Spirit
- Ask for specific gifts, with the understanding that the Holy Spirit distributes these as God leads.
- Ask to be released in the gifts, and to have the ability to recognise them in operation.
- Understand that faith and boldness are required to operate in any of the gifts.
- See the need, and ask for the specific gifts that are required; allow God's grace in their application.

Application:
The baptism of the Holy Spirit always brings about a change in people's lives. This might include greater boldness to witness, increased sensitivity to the Holy Spirit's presence, signs accompanying,[34] and other evidence. Being part of a well-taught church that has a loving and nurturing ethos will help growth and development.

Testimony:

The fire fell and burned in me till the Holy Spirit clearly revealed absolute purity before God. At this point she was called out of the room, and during her absence a marvellous revelation took place, my body became full of light and Holy Presence, and in the revelation I saw an empty Cross and at the same time the Jesus I loved and adored crowned in the Glory in a Reigning Position. The glorious remembrance of these moments is beyond my expression to give when I could not find words to express, then an irresistible Power filled me and moved my being till I found to my glorious astonishment I was speaking in other tongues clearly. After this a burning love for everybody filled my soul. I am overjoyed in giving my testimony, praying for those that fight this truth, but I am clearly given to understand that I must come out of every unbelieving element. I am already witness of signs following. Praise Him.

Smith Wigglesworth[35]

Prayer/Action:

Lord, we ask that you come in power and fill us with your Holy Spirit. May your fire fall and impart new power, zeal and boldness. Pour out the Holy Spirit upon us so that we may fulfil your purposes. Please also release in each person the gifts of the Holy Spirit so that we see your kingdom come through us. Help us to yield our lives to you. Please use each individual for your glory. In Jesus' name. Amen.

Quote:

Many saints cannot distinguish inspiration from emotion. Actually, these two can be defined readily. Emotion always enters from man's outside, whereas inspiration originates with the Holy Spirit in man's spirit.

Watchman Nee[36]

Guide 10

How to: Pray in a designated space, including setting one up

Preparation

The aim:

The aim of this guide is to help with prayer by providing a designated space within a place of worship, either temporarily or permanently. A prayer room is an opportunity to draw aside, take time out and meet with God. It is a dedicated space where people can go to pray and seek God, to intercede and petition.

Jesus withdrew to pray.

> When Jesus heard what had happened, he withdrew by boat privately to a solitary place. Hearing of this, the crowds followed him on foot from the towns. (Matthew 14:13)

> While Jesus was in one of the towns, a man came along who was covered with leprosy. When he saw Jesus, he fell with his face to the ground and begged him, 'Lord, if you are willing, you can make me clean.' Jesus reached out his hand and touched the man. 'I am willing,' he said. 'Be clean!' And immediately the leprosy left him. Then Jesus ordered him, 'Don't tell anyone, but go, show yourself to the priest and offer the sacrifices that Moses commanded for your cleansing, as a testimony to them.' Yet the news about him spread all the more, so that crowds of people came to hear him and to be healed of their illnesses. But Jesus often withdrew to lonely places and prayed.
> (Luke 5:12-16)

After the people saw the sign Jesus performed, they began to say, 'Surely this is the Prophet who is to come into the world.' Jesus, knowing that they intended to come and make him king by force, withdrew again to a mountain by himself.
(John 6:14-16)

This was not at the expense of serving the Father actively, but to be more effective in serving in the power of the Holy Spirit. Jesus seems to have really valued having a quieter place to spend time alone with His Father. This is a lesson for all of us, to find, or provide, an allocated space set aside to spend time alone with God.

What is needed:
The key is not about the physical space but about making space for a relationship with God, who from the beginning of time longs to be with his people and connect with them. We know that God is everywhere, and we can meet with God anywhere, but a prayer room with time and place set aside can be an important part of growing in relationship with God. It is a great addition to continual prayer in local church life; it can be helpful being in a place with no distractions, where the focus is on prayer.

Engaging and understanding:
A prayer room is a great way to enable regular, consistent prayer, and also provides a designated space for a 24/7 week of prayer. A prayer room model is simple and flexible. You need a space, inspiration for prayer, creative materials and people willing to pray. For 24/7 prayer in a designated space, people can do one-hour shifts, around the clock. Churches, families and communities can pray at any time, or 24/7 when you have a specific space that is set aside. Countless people have emerged from prayer rooms to report that God spoke to them in life-changing ways, that they found prayer easier, or that an hour

felt like ten minutes. Even those who do not consider themselves Christians have often experienced God's presence in such spaces.

The practicalities:
The first thing you need to organise a prayer space or room is a team! Ask God for help and look for those with a passion for prayer, creativity and organisational ability. Together, you can listen to God and motivate others, as well as design, build and run your prayer space. It is also a good idea to gather a group of people willing to be in an 'On Call Team'; people who can take responsibility for a different day – or days – of the week and leave their contact details in the room in case of a problem.

Keys to effectiveness:
Here are some simple ways to achieve an effective, designated prayer space.

- *Theme:* It is good to be clear about why you are praying. What is God asking you and your church to pray about and to pray for? Perhaps you could create a theme around the prayer room.
- *Space:* Ask for permission first, but find a space or room that you can set up for prayer.
- *Find people:* Creative, artistic people will be used to working in a range of materials and media. Ask them to help you create zones and themes conducive to prayer.
- *When:* Decide when you will pray and for how long. Then divide the time into one-hour sessions that anyone can sign up for. An hour seems a long time, but encourage people that there will be lots of prayer points, different ways/things to pray about and space to wait on God, or sit and pray quietly for the hour. Many will be blessed and inspired with an opportunity to meet with God in new ways.

- *Special occasions:* There are some key calendar dates that can be emphasised, such as Lent, Easter, Pentecost, harvest and Christmas. Seasonal focus can have a real impact in helping build a corporate prayer momentum and ownership by individuals and groups of people in church.
- *Top tip:* Have a prayer journal available in the room to collect people's written prayers and reflections.

Remember, God can make things can happen in designated spaces: Acts 2:1-2 Pentecost; 2 Chronicles 7:1-2 Shekinah glory in the house.

Activation

Biblical perspective:

And when you pray, do not be like the hypocrites, for they love to pray standing in the synagogues and on the street corners to be seen by others. Truly I tell you, they have received their reward in full. But when you pray, go into your room, close the door and pray to your Father, who is unseen. Then your Father, who sees what is done in secret, will reward you.
(Matthew 6:5-6)

Then the apostles returned to Jerusalem from the hill called the Mount of Olives, a Sabbath day's walk from the city. When they arrived, they went upstairs to the room where they were staying. Those present were Peter, John, James and Andrew; Philip and Thomas, Bartholomew and Matthew; James son of Alphaeus and Simon the Zealot, and Judas son of James. They all joined together constantly in prayer, along with the women and Mary the mother of Jesus, and with his brothers. (Acts 1:12-14)

Rejoice always, pray continually, give thanks in all circumstances; for this is God's will for you in Christ Jesus.
(1 Thessalonians 5:16-18)

Prayer points:
In this guide you are not praying for the space itself. However, you can invite the Holy Spirit to be present in the room. More importantly you can pray that the people who use the space will find it stimulating, restful and conducive to listen, and to pray in. Most people are used to praying in a plain, multi-purpose room. Here, we are trying to encourage the adaption of space to help bring additional awareness and sensitivity that comes when all our five senses are stimulated. Practical application for the increased sensitivity of our senses may include the following:

Application:
If you have selected a theme, space and timescale, what do you fill it with?

Make up several prayer stations/spaces (the number is up to you). What is a prayer station? A prayer station is an installation with something to look at or do that provokes/inspires prayer and personal reflection. Prayer stations are usually flexible and open, and yet they do need some structure so that participants can engage with them easily and confidently. For example:

- Have an explanation about the station itself: 'This is a prayer wall. Prayer can take many forms...'
- Give directions/instructions: 'Take a piece of cardboard...' 'Stop and breathe slowly...' 'Look at yourself in the mirror...'
- Have questions that encourage reflection: 'How did you feel when...?' 'What do you think this might tell you about...?' 'What is God saying...?'

- Give encouragement, quotes from people, quotes from the Bible etc. around the prayer station theme. Gather ideas together. Ask: 'Is this simple and understandable?' 'Will this help people to participate?' 'Is this prayerful?' 'Will this help people engage with God in prayer?' If yes, go for it.
- Use pictures, paintings, posters, curtains, lights, candles, scriptural symbols (for example, a cross) and other visual aids.
- Use background worship. Using a variety of different sound systems can create a peaceful atmosphere.

There are some great additional resources that can be found online See www.24-7prayer.com/prayer.

Testimony:

During my years in pastoral leadership and ministry, I have gone through many seasons of prayer and fasting. These have always seemed to be timely and influential in the life of the church. These times have been full of variety, and I remember on more than one occasion, during combined church gatherings, that each church created spaces to pray that were different. Each and every one of the church groups prepared a different emphasis, some quiet and reflective, and others having continuous worship, energy and activity. The benefits were profound. Some whose prayer meetings were always full of worship and fervent praying were deeply impacted by opportunities to sit quietly and listen to God. It was amazing how God spoke in the stillness, whilst people were looking at the helpful imagery, worksheets and use of light textures. I learned that God is creative, and he has made us capable of developing imaginative places for us to meet with him. Inevitably, we heard from God in fresh ways that have helped shaped the church, and brought greater fruitfulness.

Roger Grassham

Prayer/Action:
Lord, we thank you for direct access to you through prayer. Please help us to develop a regular, daily prayer life that brings us closer to you, and increases our understanding of what you think (your thoughts), and what you want us to do (your ways). Help us to recognise that the prayer of faith will enable us to do extraordinary supernatural things to see transformation in people's lives. Give us the strength, perseverance and courage to stand 'in the gap', to watch, and to pray. In Jesus' name. Amen.

Quote:

True prayer is neither a mere mental exercise nor a vocal performance. It is far deeper than that – it is spiritual transaction with the Creator of Heaven and Earth.

Charles Spurgeon[37]

Guide 11

How to: Pray for God's presence in worship and the prophetic

Preparation

The aim:

The aim of this guide is to give some useful insight and help as we pray for God to be tangibly present as we worship him. In our praise and worship, there is an amazing level of creativity possible as we are open to the release of the gifts of the Holy Spirit, especially through dreams, visions and prophetic words. The foundation of truth in the Scriptures (*Logos*) comes alive as the Holy Spirit leads us to read and declare passages of God's Word (*Rhema*). This isn't so much about feelings, it's more about sensing the breath of God bringing change so that we become sensitively conscious of his presence. In this guide there are some keys to help create an atmosphere conducive to a manifestation of God's presence. During prayer there are precious moments where an intimacy and knowledge of the Holy Spirit is developed, when evidence of His presence comes, with the awareness of the Shekinah glory of God. At these times, the gifts of the Holy Spirit are often released, and fresh inspiration becomes evident.

What is needed:

Prayer, worship and prophetic gatherings of any size are most effective when we verbalise our adoration of the Lord and open our hearts for God to move in us supernaturally. Having our full focus on the Lord creates space for the intimate presence of the Holy Spirit in every gathering. We need to prepare our hearts beforehand and to be open to the promptings of the Holy Spirit individually. When we all do this, the potential for God's presence increases exponentially, thus releasing the refreshing wells of 'living water' within us (John 7:38).

Engaging and understanding:
Jesus spent time with his Father alone, and from this intimate relationship, moved in the power of the Holy Spirit and taught the people, accompanied by many supernatural signs. How much more important is it for us to prepare our hearts. In the Old Testament, we read of the High Priest ministering to the Lord in the Holy of Holies (Hebrews 9:7). He wore a robe with bells and pomegranates sown into the hem of the garment (Exodus 28:34). Such was the intensity of God's glory in the holy of holies, hearing the bells ring reassured the people that the High Priest was alive and well. As we are priests of the Lord under the New Covenant, the Holy Spirit imparts gifts and fruit (Galatians 5:22-23) to enable us to minister with anointing in his power. It is therefore very important that we are fully prepared in terms of our walk with God, which I outline more in the next section. The Bible tells us the Shekinah glory was seen over the tabernacle Holy of Holies (Exodus 19:16-18). When we worship, pray and are open to the moving of the Holy Spirit, the presence of God will be clearly evident.

The practicalities:
It is important to understand the kind of lifestyle that God looks for when entrusting his divine presence to come among his people.

- *Clean hands:* '... Who may stand in his holy place? The one who has clean hands and a pure heart ...' (Psalm 24:3-4)
- *Purity*: 'Create in me a pure heart, O God, and renew a steadfast spirit within me' (Psalm 51:10).

- *Holiness*: 'Worship the LORD in the splendour of his holiness; tremble before him, all the earth' (Psalm 96:9).
- *Fear of the Lord*: 'The Spirit of the LORD will rest on him … the Spirit of the … fear of the LORD' (Isaiah 11:2).
- *Love God:* 'Love the Lord your God with all your heart and with all your soul and with all your mind' (Matthew 22:37).
- *Love his Word:* 'Your word is a lamp for my feet, a light on my path' (Psalm 119:105).
- *Love to worship:* 'Exalt the LORD our God and worship at his footstool; he is holy' (Psalm 99:5).
- *Love to pray:* 'Rejoice always, pray continually, give thanks in all circumstances' (1 Thessalonians 5:16-18).
- *Prophecy:* 'Follow the way of love and eagerly desire gifts of the Spirit, especially prophecy' (1 Corinthians 14:1).

Keys to effectiveness:
In preparation we must actively desire these key areas:

- *Total dependence on the Lord.* 'So he said to me, "This is the word of the LORD to Zerubbabel: 'Not by might nor by power, but by my Spirit,' says the LORD Almighty' (Zechariah 4:6).
- *Love of the truth:* 'This is what the LORD Almighty says: … Therefore, love truth and peace' (Zechariah 8:19).
- *Love people:* 'A new command I give you: … As I have loved you, so you must love one another' (John 13:34).
- *Righteousness:* 'You love righteousness and hate wickedness … anointing you with the oil of joy' (Psalm 45:7).
- *Be dependable:* 'Commit your way to the LORD; trust in him and he will do this' (Psalm 37:5).

Activation

Biblical perspective:

The Lord replied, 'My Presence will go with you, and I will give you rest.'
(Exodus 33:14)

Create in me a pure heart, O God, and renew a steadfast spirit within me. Do not cast me from your presence or take your Holy Spirit from me.
(Psalm 51:10-11)

Where can I go from your Spirit? Where can I flee from your presence?
(Psalm 139:7)

Therefore, brothers and sisters, since we have confidence to enter the Most Holy Place by the blood of Jesus, by a new and living way opened for us through the curtain, that is, his body, and since we have a great priest over the house of God, let us draw near to God with a sincere heart and with the full assurance that faith brings, having our hearts ... washed with pure water.
(Hebrews 10:19-22)

Prayer points:
Find a place to seek God's face. Find a posture that helps you as you submit to God. Open your heart, worship him, pray and ask God to manifest his presence in the following ways.

- *Ask* that the Lord would visit you, and make his intimate presence known in your life.

- *Use your faith* to believe that he can change you through prayer, love and his heart for you.
- *Pray* that his kingdom be revealed in tangible ways. Remember the power and glory are God's alone.[38]
- *Cultivate* his presence in your life and centre your wandering thoughts on him.
- *As you yield* to God, allow him to transform you as you pray, worship and listen to his Spirit.
- *Remove* any distractions that keep you from his presence, and repent of allowing them in.
- *Ask* God to show you your spiritual identity in him. As you pray and reach out to him, ask him to show you how to use the authority we have in Christ.
- *Desire* to be clean. Fill your heart and mind with God's Word and allow his presence in every area.
- *Let God* lead you up higher, around his throne. Have a desire to sit with him in heavenly places.
- *Desire* to worship only God. Ask him to show you how to go deeper in prayer and intimacy with him.
- *Ask* God to help you walk in light and holiness. Have a deep desire to know him more.
- *Rejoice* in his presence so that his joy overflows into the lives of others.
- *Ask* God to implant a desire to dwell in his house, to gaze on his beauty and to seek His face – Psalm 27:4.
- *Ask* the Holy Spirit to release dreams, visions and scriptures. Share them and watch God confirm their interpretation through people. Be prepared for God to lead you to prophetic acts, which will test and stretch faith. Prophetic acts means acting on prophecy by initiating practical acts that are symbolic of obedience to what God has said inspirationally;

for example, putting scripture texts in a bottle and building them into a wall, or putting oil onto the lintel of a strategic doorway. This sort of thing might seem strange, but takes faith and trust to do it.

Application:

Our desire is to live in and daily to experience the presence of God. Praying and worshipping in the Holy Spirit builds a platform for God to release the gifts of the Holy Spirit. Speaking and singing in tongues allows his Spirit to flow through us, bypassing our mind, which sometimes gets in the way. Preparation is everything, but the Holy Spirit will often interrupt our plans and lead us differently. Learn to be sensitive to the Spirit. Learn how to administer the gifts of the Holy Spirit. For this to happen, let us be prepared in our hearts and minds to receive from God by doing these three things:

1. Spending *time*, listening to God, attuning to his voice in our thoughts, and by being led to find scripture and inspiration because we have quietened our heart and slowed our pace.
2. Using *space*, by putting ourselves into a physical setting that is conducive to hearing from God. This can be inside, outside, or somewhere that is a special place to us, and where we may have heard God speaking to us before.
3. Facilitating *freedom*, by listening to worship, teaching and prophetic utterances that stimulate and release us spiritually.

All three areas are extremely useful in order to experience release and breakthrough in the flow of the Holy Spirit.

Testimony:

It is not unusual for me to sense the presence of God by sitting quietly at the breakfast table with worship music playing in the background. It is amazing how the Holy Spirit quickens a particular song and I start to feel God's voice reminding me that he is there. In those moments I remember the unexpected events of the past weeks, the conversations that have had significant emotion attached to them, and associated challenges. If I am prepared to be vulnerable in those moments, tears will flow, a strong spiritual embrace ensues, and God's comfort and reassurance is apparent. My spirit is lifted in those times, which results in a new perspective. If I am prepared to give God a bit of extra time, words and phrases, scriptures and pictures flow into my mind and heart. I write these down on whatever means I have to hand. Often, a few days later, the relevance of what God spoke to me becomes clear, and I use it to bless someone in need. I have discovered that vulnerability and transparency and honesty with God leads to a sure knowledge of his presence. I am so grateful to God for these times and pray these experiences never go away. That can be down to my choices!

Roger Grassham

Prayer/Action:

Lord, we need more of you in our lives. As we worship, adore and bow before you, we desire your presence in our lives. Release a fresh, new outpouring of your power and love as we draw close to you. May your Holy Spirit bring fresh revelation, love and compassion, so that others may find you and know you for themselves. Amen.

Quote:

When we come to the place of impossibilities, it is the grandest
place for us to see the possibilities of God.
Smith Wigglesworth[39]

Guide 12

How to: Pray for young people and families across the generations

Preparation

The aim:

The aim of this guide is to help understanding and how to pray for young people and their families as they mature and grow. This guide builds on Guide 6 – prayer for children and young people.

Most people in their twenties and above will marry and have families of their own, thus creating new generations. It is worth noting how important it is to recognise that some young people remain single by choice, and some due to circumstances. Parents become grandparents and sometimes great-grandparents. Everyone is part of a generational family legacy, regardless of our backgrounds.

What is needed:

There is a real need for society to remain committed to marriage and the family as an essential foundation. With the changes in laws, equality policies and government-led educational pressure, the very fabric of family make-up and understanding of what constitutes family is under pressure. These changes are challenging. Families are forced to adapt and change their understanding. There is a need for the Church to teach Bible principles and provide guidance on how to build healthy relationships within families of all generations. Advice and support for struggling families is essential. Some experiences within families are not positive ones. We must always be sensitive to the impact on those people adversely affected, and who will often need help reforming views and opinions on role models.

Engaging and understanding:
The importance of praying for young people and families generationally cannot be underestimated. Effective prayer is needed for people's spiritual awareness, growth and development. We also need to consider external factors in society that influence people. These include positive and negative elements, such as:

Positive
- good role models in parents and siblings in the extended family and friendships;
- a supportive, affirming and encouraging home environment that urges the fulfilment of potential;
- a loving and appreciative atmosphere where family members are devoted to supporting one another;
- a generous and warm-hearted attitude that pervades day-to-day life at home and elsewhere;
- a God-fearing lifestyle due to a strong Christian upbringing and involvement in church life, and people whose character has become something to look up to;
- strong marriages and stable relationships through the generations;
- evidence of positive characteristics in individual family members that are passed on generationally.

Negative
- not having any Christian influence in the home or knowledge of God at any level in family upbringing;
- having only basic knowledge of Christianity through church attendance being limited to weddings, funerals, and christenings;

- having a background of faith that is not Christian in origin. This is likely to include ungodly religious rituals and culture;
- having bad experiences in upbringing of suffering because of external influences, as well as hindrances to achieving goals;
- love based solely on relation to possessions, money, status and/or family pride;
- health issues that affect family members, the family structure and expression;
- breakdowns in relationships that leave lasting scars of hurt and misunderstanding in the family.
- the Bible speaks about iniquity, and its consequences which affect the third and fourth generations (Exodus 34:7; Deuteronomy 5:9; Numbers 2:14:18). My experience has shown that repentance and prayer loosens the hold of any curses and strongholds.

The practicalities:

When praying about young people and families, there is often a history of stories that get passed on from generation to generation. Some will be positive and some will be negative and others, just funny! In wanting to pray meaningfully for young people and their families, it is important to try to understand the key factors that either make for solid family relationships or why some families struggle to establish loving relationships. Understanding that people's experiences in families are all very different, great sensitivity is needed as we pray. Always use wisdom, and adjust phraseology accordingly. Remember that in some cases, there are likely to be long-lasting, painful fractures and relational separations that affect some young people and their families.

Keys to effectiveness:

- Think carefully about the internal and external factors that can have an impact on families.
- Prayerfully consider the strategies that build strong bonds and pressures that create tension.
- Consider what the Bible has to say about a godly lifestyle when it comes to generational blessing. See 1 Timothy 4:7.
- Ask people to be honest about generational traits and influences on them. It will help to be informed.

Activation

Biblical perspective:

Listen, my son, accept what I say, and the years of your life will be many. I instruct you in the way of wisdom and lead you along straight paths. When you walk, your steps will not be hampered; when you run, you will not stumble. Hold on to instruction, do not let it go; guard it well, for it is your life. Do not set foot on the path of the wicked or walk in the way of evildoers. Avoid it, do not travel on it; turn from it and go on your way.
(Proverbs 4:10-15)

And God said, 'This is the sign of the covenant I am making between me and you and every living creature with you, a covenant for all generations to come: I have set my rainbow in the clouds, and it will be the sign of the covenant between me and the earth.
(Genesis 9:12-13)

The promise is for you and your children and for all who are far off – for all whom the Lord our God will call.
(Acts 2:39)

Prayer points:
Ask God to give a generational blessing to young people and their families for generations to come. Pray that those without Christ leave their past life behind them, and ask God to forgive sin and then yield their lives to the lordship of Jesus. Pray they will also experience transformation in their families. Pray, specifically that

- young people will be respectful, and desire to live lives free of things that draw them away from God's ways;
- young people studying in universities and colleges or doing apprenticeships will be wise in friendship choices;
- young people will have a respect for marriage and family and become committed in relationships that glorify God;
- young families become stable, healthy and affirming places, so that children grow and mature well;
- as parents become grandparents, they will continue to value and respect each generation;
- youth and families that are dysfunctional will receive healing, and come to know God's grace and peace as they deal with issues;
- God's love will be released to bring reconciliation and healing in families where relationships are strained;
- any limitations, barriers and unhelpful lifestyle patterns will be broken in the name of Jesus;
- the blessing of God will rest on those that seek to walk in obedience to his Word;
- when families and generations experience challenges, they will come to know God's grace, freedom and healing;

- every individual and family would fulfil their potential and destiny in God's purposes in every area.

Application:

Young people and families have generational history, some of which will be good and some more difficult to live with. Regardless, God desires everyone to come to the knowledge of the truth in Christ Jesus. In Christ is life, freedom and joy in the Holy Spirit. God's power can break anyone free from curses, bad reputations, or generational traits that try to hinder a walk of discipleship. Nothing is impossible to God.[40]

Testimony:

I was brought up in a loving, Christian home, for which I am really grateful. I found Jesus as Lord and Saviour when incredibly young. As a teenager I drifted, had a battle of wills with the Lord regarding my priorities and felt a failure. God intervened and in my early twenties I repented and was baptised in the Holy Spirit. I then tried to obey God in everything. I married and had children and felt blessed and grateful for God's restoration. My wife and I navigated the pressure of life and church leadership. Some circumstances seemed unusually difficult to deal with. Tension, stress and a spiritual battle took its toll. We asked pastoral leaders for prayer and ministry. The curse of generational bondage was discerned (similar to being spiritually enslaved), and its power broken off us.[41] The result was dramatic. Our relationship improved in every way. We continue to praise God. We are now grandparents, and all our family continues to serve God.

Roger Grassham

Prayer/Action:
Lord, please bring unlimited blessings on the family generations. Help the young people and family members to seek to obey and follow in all your ways. Please intervene in the lives of families who do not know you and help them find the true and living way. Please release and heal those young people and families who struggle in their relationships and lead them into freedom, peace and reconciliation. In Jesus' name. Amen.

Quote:

We have come to a turning point in the road. If we turn to the right mayhap our children and our children's children will go that way; but if we turn to the left, generations yet unborn will curse our names for having been unfaithful to God and to His Word.

Charles Spurgeon[42]

Guide 13

How to: Pray as you walk

Preparation

The aim:

The aim of this guide is to help you think about how to pray while walking on the streets of our community. This sort of prayer is really about carrying the presence of God into where we live, work and go to church geographically. The guide sets out a few strategic ways in which we can gain greater insight and understanding into the spiritual influences that may be in place, and then find God's key to bring release and transformation.

What is needed:

Praying as we walk is helpful, especially when we can see, hear and feel the atmosphere. This allows God to bring revelation and understanding about our community, and the forces at work to disrupt and negatively control people's lives (Jeremiah 33:2-3).

If you have a burden to pray for your neighbours, your village, town, or city, venturing out onto the streets and exploring is helpful in building a picture of the demographic make-up. The sort of things that will be needed to help you pray effectively are as follows.

- Research the local area's history and go back 100 years or more to gather as much information as possible.
- Find out if there have been any significant events that have affected the area.
- Look at press records to see whether there have been influential people who have impacted community life.

- Discover if there have been any organisations that have brought philosophical or religious thought.
- See if there have been any accidents, disasters, events, or decisions affecting people's lives.
- Go to the library, search online or read books or articles about local history.

Engaging and understanding:
God has a plan and destiny for every person, but also for every place. He is interested in the well-being of people, but in localities too. There are many examples in the Bible that speak about God's people moving into territory that he had ordained for them to occupy and possess as an inheritance (Jeremiah 29:7). This is commonly called 'spiritual mapping' in some churches that are from a charismatic or Pentecostal persuasion. Intercessors and community members will often find valuable information when looking at historical research into an area. Simply put, spiritual mapping is the process of prayerfully building up a picture of a location based on the influences affecting it. Whatever we may call it, tracing the key factors that influence localities is important so that we can pray in an informed manner.

The practicalities:
Preparation is essential. Ask God for insights. Spiritual alertness is more important than buildings and the landscape. Find out about local disputes, strikes and/or protests. Look for motives for the founding of businesses or other institutions. Approach street praying with an open heart. Listen to promptings of the Holy Spirit. Let God bring dreams, visions, scriptures, prophetic words and strong impressions. Be self-aware as you walk, and behave wisely (Ephesians 6:18). Consider going out in pairs. Decide whether you want to stay

silent and listen, or pray quietly as you walk. If you are praying as part of a larger group, start together and finish together. Give feedback and take notes. Use maps and mark them up.

Keys to effectiveness:
Some of the keys to effective praying about a place include the following examples of cause and effect:

- empty shops, high unemployment and rough sleeping caused by inequalities and social exclusion;
- slave trading, sex working, gambling because of poverty, deprivation and underachievement;
- graffiti on walls caused by the need to express dissatisfaction with those who have power and influence;
- poor health accompanied by poor educational achievement caused by low esteem and expectations;
- antisocial behaviour with gangs caused by family breakdown and dysfunctional lifestyles;
- addiction to substances caused by a mixture of all the above and a lack of purpose in life;
- mental health, depression, disorders and difficult behavioural patterns caused by traumatic experiences.

Note:

- Larger towns and cities may have higher proportions of issues mentioned in this list.
- Research will help in your understanding.
- Spiritual discernment and prophetic prayer will help bring some of the answers.
- You may have heard the phrase 'marrying the land' (Isaiah

62:4)? It has been used to describe a covenant of prayerful personal engagement in a town or city, reminding us of commitment and full engagement in community transformation over an extended period of time.

Activation

Biblical perspective:

The LORD said to Moses, 'Send some men to explore the land of Canaan, which I am giving to the Israelites. From each ancestral tribe send one of its leaders.' So at the LORD's command Moses sent them out from the Desert of Paran. ...
(Numbers 13:1-3)

Also, seek the peace and prosperity of the city to which I have carried you into exile. Pray to the LORD for it, because if it prospers, you too will prosper.
(Jeremiah 29:7)

For Zion's sake I will not keep silent, for Jerusalem's sake I will not remain quiet, till her vindication shines out like the dawn, her salvation like a blazing torch. The nations will see your vindication, and all kings your glory; you will be called by a new name that the mouth of the LORD will bestow. You will be a crown of splendour in the LORD's hand, a royal diadem in the hand of your God. No longer will they call you Deserted, or name your land Desolate. But you will be called Hephzibah, and your land Beulah; for the LORD will take delight in you, and your land will be married.
(Isaiah 62:1-4)

Live in harmony with one another. Do not be proud, but be willing to associate with people of low position. Do not be conceited.
(Romans 12:16)

Prayer points:
Here are a number of ways to pray, and to respond to promptings as you walk.

- Pray before you go out, and ask a few people to pray for your protection and covering as you go.
- Pray in the Spirit (i.e. in tongues) as you walk, as well as with ordinary language. Ask God to show you things you may not have seen before.
- Ask the Holy Spirit to give you sensitivity at road and rail junctions, special places and notable buildings or structures.
- Let the Holy Spirit reveal anything that might be hidden underground in foundations and at deeper levels (for example, things that people might have buried, old buriel grounds, places where significant actions were taken in history and underground streams that can either have scriptural significance or pagan symbolism, etc.).
- As you pray, if you sense turmoil, speak the peace of Jesus to that place, that it may impact people affected.
- Ask God to cleanse the atmosphere, and cleanse the district of addiction to drugs and other things, speak freedom and the loosing of chains of bondage. Also, that God will expose the powers of darkness and the perpetrators be found.
- If you sense grief or distress, consider pausing, and put some oil on a post or suitable place to declare an anointing as you pray for joy and peace to prevail.

- As you pray you may feel led to sprinkle water and/or salt. Here is why:

  The people of the city said to Elisha, 'Look, our lord … the water is bad and the land is unproductive.' 'Bring me a new bowl,' he said, 'and put salt in it.' So they brought it to him. Then he … threw the salt into it, saying, 'This is what the LORD says: "I have healed this water. Never again will it cause death or make the land unproductive."'
  (2 Kings 2:19-21)

- Prophetic acts. This will mean carrying out practical things arising directly from any words of prophecy. They may be symbolic and underline obedience to God; for example, putting scripture in a container and building it into a wall, or putting oil on the lintel of a strategic doorway.
- Pray about the atmosphere, airwaves and positive and negative language used on the streets.
- Pray for a spirit of generosity, kindness and patience to be poured out on your community.
- Because of your research, you will uncover negative things. Pray in the opposite spirit, declaring the peace of God to prevail.
- More than anything, as you pray, allow the Holy Spirit to bring revelation, inspiration and insight everywhere.

Application:
There are so many practical things that God uses alongside regular, fervent prayer. Prayer is so much more than using words to talk to God.

- It is *listening* to the promptings of the Holy Spirit and *acting* on what he says.

- It is *asking* God for revelation and watching him *provide* the insights.
- It is *going* where he tells you to go and *discovering* why.
- It is *responding* to God's leading and *doing something* with the information, by faith.

Testimony:

In Canning Town in east London, the area around the church where I served was very run down and deteriorating badly. The church prayer group and intercessors periodically left the building and walked the streets praying for God to radically transform the area. Demolition of old buildings and a lack of investment and maintenance had made the area unsafe. After a few years, the church decided to put on a special 'Alive' weekend of evangelism, outreach and community action. Dozens of church members cleared rubbish, cut grass, removed graffiti and repainted walls with murals, planted new flowers and generally tidied the area. The run-down park near the church nursery was transformed. The local council took note and reintroduced regular maintenance. To this day the area is better kept than ever it was previously.

Roger Grassham

Prayer/Action:

Lord, as we go into the community to pray, please will you give us 'everywhere we put our feet', just as you did with Joshua.[43] Guide us as we respond to, and act upon, the leadings of the Holy Spirit in practical ways. Show us what we can do to influence planning and decisions that will affect our community. Please reveal your strategies to pray and reclaim territory, in Jesus' name. Amen.

Quote:

Effective mission can only be conducted through prayer and a total reliance upon the power and dynamic of the Holy Spirit. Alistair Cole[44]

Guide 14

How to: Pray for the prodigals

Preparation

The aim:

The aim of this guide is to help in praying for those people whose love for God has grown cold, and for those who have walked away from him either by choice or because of circumstances. The term 'prodigals' comes from the story about the son who walked away from his father in Luke 15.

Many prodigals will have struggled with hurt, grief and loss and possibly disillusionment. God still loves them, and so praying for repentance, healing and renewal is part of their restoration.

What is needed:

To see the return of prodigals we must set aside any pre-judgement of people's lives. God loves each person as an individual, despite their having possibly disobeyed God or just drifted away due to painful experiences. Seeing people as our heavenly Father sees them is essential in helping us be compassionate and not critical. None of us know the reasons why people fall away and 'backslide', a term used for drifting away from God.[45] To pray effectively, we need to ask God to soften our hearts and let the Holy Spirit express God's heart through us to restore, rebuild and renew each prodigal's life.

Engaging and understanding:

All will know someone who has had bad experiences and consequently drifted away from church. Prodigals will often be people who have previously been actively involved in Christian life. There may have been disagreements in relationships, different experiences of teaching and preaching or feelings of rejection. It may be that a family or church bereavement has affected someone badly. In some cases, people have allowed worldly thinking and philosophy to creep in and undermine faith. For some, a cynical attitude has developed due to perceptions of hypocrisy. Whatever the reason, God still loves these people and wants them to be restored to a relationship with him.

The practicalities:
Praying for someone who has been deeply hurt means asking for God to heal that person's wounded heart. Fear of rejection may be a real issue for someone, so a safe place among kind people will be needed. A person who has been deceived or got themselves entangled with other philosophies or religions will need to hear truth shared with love.[46] Those who have been grieving will need hope and the promise of a future. Seek God in prayer for a supernatural love and keen spiritual instinct with words of knowledge, wisdom and discernment.[47] Here are some keys to help pray effectively:

Keys to effectiveness:
There are so many different reasons why people have fallen or drifted away from discipleship.

- *Think* about people who may have left your church. If possible, find out their names.
- *Diplomatically* find out why people have left, to ensure there are no future relational obstacles.
- *Have* a discerning heart that is compassionate, but also understanding of God's truths.

- *Be prepared* to face up to and understand why people drift away from God.
- *Allow* God supernaturally to reveal causes and influences affecting prodigals.
- *When* people reappear after a long absence, be a good listener to their experiences.
- *Understand* that some people will be broken and damaged. Prepare your heart.
- *Family* members might be estranged from one another as well as from faith.
- *Hardness* of heart may have crept into some people's lives; only God can soften them.

Activation

Biblical perspective:

So he got up and went to his father. But while he was still a long way off, his father saw him and was filled with compassion for him; he ran to his son, threw his arms round him and kissed him. The son said to him, 'Father, I have sinned against heaven and against you. I am no longer worthy to be called your son.' But the father said to his servants, 'Quick! Bring the best robe and put it on him. Put a ring on his finger and sandals on his feet. Bring the fattened calf and kill it. Let's have a feast and celebrate. For this son of mine was dead and is alive again; he was lost and is found.' So they began to celebrate.
(Luke 15:20-24)

Prayer points:
The parable of Jesus in Luke 15 is helpful in showing how to pray for prodigals. Pray that they would return to God and that those affected have open hearts to be restored. Pray that there will be:

- acknowledgement about wrong life choices, and a need for humility;
- a recognition about challenging circumstances that has caused them to be estranged relationally;
- an acceptance that there has been emotional reaction against authority and a need for repentance;
- an openness to being convicted in the heart, realising their need of reconciliation and reconnection with family;
- a realisation of wrongdoing and ownership of their part in the breakdown in relationship;
- a need for a repentant heart even if there has been injustice, and an openness to restoration with people who have been hurt and have caused hurt;
- a softening of heart and mind to help facilitate restoration by anyone affected by the prodigal's decisions and actions;
- love and warmth in the hearts and minds of everyone involved;
- healing in spirit, soul and body and a renewal of personal relationships;
- an openness to be reintroduced to the church family, and be lovingly restored, discipled and mutually befriended as part of the restoration process.

Application:

Prodigals will invariably have:

- been misunderstood by people;
- experienced rejection by people they have put their trust in as friends;
- made mistakes and feel a sense of shame;
- felt confused and been influenced by unhelpful people outside their normal friendship group;
- become trapped by a myriad of complicated circumstances;
- become disillusioned by the way they have been treated;
- been put off by the inappropriate behaviour of people they have previously respected.

In the mixture of different life experiences, some prodigals may have had experiences outside of the kingdom of God, requiring healing, with great love and understanding. It takes time to become re-established, renewed and realigned to God's ways. It will be necessary for everyone not to be judgemental about the prodigal's past but understand the amazing saving grace that is offered by God to those who are restored. Depending on the circumstances, talk openly and pray sensitively about issues with wisdom, tact and spiritual insight.

Testimony:

When I think back to my teenage years, it pains me to think just how ignorant and vulnerable I was to face the big wide world. I was in a bubble of Christian people, particularly my own family. Our lifestyle was very committed and busy within the local church I attended, my having become a Christian at the age of seven. It is fair to say I started to experiment and push boundaries. This resulted in my starting to investigate what other people were doing outside the church. In particular, when I got a job at the BBC in the West End of London, I started to be affected by colleagues' attitudes, morality and lifestyles. During the week I started to party and drink. This in itself was bad news at the time, because I had signed a pledge to be teetotal within my church denomination. I got close to alcohol dependency, nearly crossed boundaries in relationships, and experienced some abuse.

All of this started to get to me mentally and emotionally. I got depressed and had to take over-the-counter medication to deal with headaches and stress. I was at further education college to try to catch up academically, as I had failed at secondary school. I sunk really low and soon realised I was living a double life. Effectively I was a hypocrite, praying and testifying at church but living a different kind of life at other times. I know my parents were worried.

I hit rock bottom aged twenty-one. I cried out to God and he heard me. Through a series of circumstances that I now know were ordained by God, I found my way back to a personal relationship with Jesus. I repented and was soon filled with the Holy Spirit by the laying on of hands (Acts 8:14-19). My life changed dramatically, and I am forever grateful to God that he never let me go, and restored me once again.
Roger Grassham

All of us can identify with periods of time in our lives when we have run away from God. This is a bit like running away from family, albeit God's own family. Let us thank God for the fact he welcomes us back with open arms when we come to our senses and repent.

Prayer/Action:
Lord, I bring to you those who have been hurt, disillusioned and made low. Some may have also turned away from you. We recognise that some people we know have become estranged from their own family, and also the Church family. We ask you to bring fresh revelation of your love and forgiveness as prodigals reach the low point and realisation of sin, separation and loneliness and the need for repentance. We also ask for your grace to be released to the relatives of those prodigals who have been estranged from them by their actions and lifestyle. Please bring healing and reconciliation with their own families too. Thank you for hearing our prayer, Lord. Amen.

Quote:

It is not reason which turns the young man from God; it is the flesh. Scepticism but provides him with the excuses for the new life he is leading.
Augustine of Hippo[48]

Guide 15

How to: Pray in a time of crisis

Preparation

The aim:

The aim of this guide is to help in prayer when we are facing a major crisis, whether it be family, church, community, or nationally. Complex issues can arise and affect us, and knowing how to respond when these occur can help bring hope, peace and a sense of community in the storm.

What is needed:

Our attitude and responses need to be centred on something solid and reassuring during a crisis. For disciples of Jesus, the hymn by Edward Mote is apt: 'My Hope is Built on Nothing Less'.[49] This is partly based on the scripture in 1 Corinthians 10:3-4: 'They all ate the same spiritual food and drank the same spiritual drink; for they drank from the spiritual rock that accompanied them, and that rock was Christ.' The truth indicates a solid rock to stand on in times of trouble. Jesus did not promise the absence of trouble, he promised to be with us in it! 'I have told you these things, so that in me you may have peace. In this world you will have trouble. But take heart! I have overcome the world' (John 16:33).

Engaging and understanding:

At the onset of an emergency or sudden unexpected event, it is sometimes hard not to panic and become stressed and fearful. At these times we need to pray and then act.

Firstly, prayer will help steady us so that we can engage with God, who will be fully aware of what we face even before we ask! In Mark 4:35-39 we see that Jesus, when hearing the disciples' fear and panic on Lake Galilee, faced the storm and rebuked it, saying, 'Quiet! Be still!' Crying out to God will bring peace.

Secondly, we need to face the issues head-on, take stock and ask God for wisdom on how to act: 'If any of you lacks wisdom, you should ask God, who gives generously to all without finding fault, and it will be given to you' (James 1:5).

Thirdly, we need to act by listening and responding to advice from those who are skilled and experienced with the specific issues.

Be sure that following these three processes will result in being loved and lifted as you act. 'Let the morning bring me word of your unfailing love, for I have put my trust in you. Show me the way I should go, for to you I entrust my life' (Psalm 143:8).

Shock and grief is something we will all face in our lives, but often will come suddenly, and without warning.

The practicalities:
People respond differently in a crisis. Regardless, there are essential things to do. If your personality stays calm and your thinking remains clear, draw from experience but call people to pray and cover you as you act. If you tend to freeze or panic, call someone with proven calmness to advise and suggest steps to help you. After the initial response to sudden events, there will come a period of reflection. It is vital during this time that you focus on God and try to see things from his perspective – He is in sovereign! He is there for you! He will never let you down. God is faithful! Jesus is the Prince of Peace: 'For to us a child is born, to us a son is given, and the government will be on his shoulders.

And he will be called Wonderful Counsellor, Mighty God, Everlasting Father, Prince of Peace' (Isaiah 9:6).

Keys to effectiveness:

There are some practical things to do when you face a crisis. Chiefly, don't try to do everything on your own! The Church is there as a family, as a fellowship of believers; they should help to share the load.

- *Reach out* to trusted fellow Christians and seek prayer and practical support.
- *Seek out advice* from reliable sources and use as a template to structure time and effort.
- *Establish* a clear routine to help you cope spiritually, in soul (mind) and in body.
- *Instinct* in crisis is to act first, but make sure prayer is prioritised before, during and after.
- *Always* seek to behave with wisdom and tact. Our hearts will determine our speech.
- *Declare* the goodness of God over you and over those affected by the crisis.
- *Communicate*, and share your concerns and burdens. Others will help you bear them.
- *Be compassionate,* and treat people with great sensitivity, especially in the early stages of unexpected events.

Activation

Biblical perspective:

There are scriptures that help us to focus and pray in a crisis:

> The righteous cry out, and the LORD hears them; he delivers them from all their troubles. The LORD is close to the broken-hearted and saves those who are crushed in spirit. The righteous person may have many troubles, but the LORD delivers him from them all …
>
> (Psalm 34:17-19)

and:

I have told you these things, so that in me you may have peace. In this world you will have trouble. But take heart! I have overcome the world.
(John 16:33)

Prayer points:
Here are some general prayer points to help pray meaningfully during a crisis, that

- those struggling with fear and anxiety would know peace that 'transcends all understanding' (Philippians 4:7);
- those with mental and emotional trauma would know they are loved, safe and secure. All those affected by shock, trauma and grief will know God's comfort and peace;
- those with responsibilities for pastoral care would know deep compassion and empathy;
- those with leadership responsibility would have a calm, creative energy to guide and inform;
- those with community and governmental oversight will rule wisely and fairly;
- those dealing with emergency response services will have all the strength and calm needed;
- those needing to deal with strategic matters – for example, factory fire or building collapse – would be able to establish teams to respond;
- those struggling with financial pressure and responsibility would see God's provision;
- those with health challenges would experience God's healing, and recover fully;

- those needing to communicate with diverse teams would be able to access the resources needed.
- those who are grieving and needing to come to terms with sudden loss of friends and loved ones will do so.

Application:

Ask God for a heart of compassion; also a steady heart to respond to needs. Be aware that people respond differently, and may display extreme reactions and responses. Comfort those who are grieving (Matthew 5:4). You may face people's anger, distress and fear because of what you represent. Do not take this personally but see things from God's perspective. Remember the words: 'A gentle answer turns away wrath, but a harsh word stirs up anger' (Proverbs 15:1). During stressful times, our attitudes and our core reactions become evident. This is a time to press into God and have grateful hearts, be open to God challenging us and then responding rather than reacting to the circumstances, especially in relationships. Look for the good and praiseworthy things in each other: 'Finally, brothers and sisters, whatever is true, whatever is noble, whatever is right, whatever is pure, whatever is lovely, whatever is admirable – if anything is excellent or praiseworthy – think about such things (Philippians 4:8).

Testimony:

Elim Pentecostal church pastor Mark McCLurg from Newtownards, NI, was directly affected by the coronavirus in 2020 during the Covid-19 pandemic. The Elim *Direction* magazine carried an article about Mark's story and this an extract from the October 2020 edition:

I prayed, 'Lord, I need your help, please heal me.' I was lying with my eyes closed listening to worship music with my right hand down the side of my body.

I felt my hand being grabbed. A nurse was at the bottom of the bed and I asked if she had held my hand, but she said she hadn't moved from her seat.

Then the Holy Spirit reminded me of when Jesus held the little girl's hand, and I realised that even if I had to go on a ventilator he was holding mine and I was going to rise from it, so I had peace.

Mark recovered in March 2020 and as he left hospital, tweeted:

I have some amazing news. I'm leaving the Ulster Hospital. I want to thank everyone for their prayers. I want to thank the staff at the Ulster Hospital for saving my life. I am looking forward to enjoying life. Overcome #Coronavirus. Be kind. Jesus is my healer.

Prayer/Action:
Lord, we call upon you for help in this crisis (name the crisis). Please pour out your grace and wisdom as we try to find the best way to respond and support people. May every person (name them if they are known to you) know your love and peace as they deal with the knock-on effects. In Jesus' name. Amen.

Quote:

As our world is confronting their mortality, for some of them the first time, we have the choice to either place our faith in the hope of Christ or to mirror their fear born of a perishable hope.
Ed Stetzer[50]

Guide 16

How to: Pray for mental and emotional health

Preparation

The aim:

The aim of this guide is to help in praying for people in our society who struggle mentally and emotionally. It is essential to have compassion, concern and consideration when we pray. Care is necessary as we address this ever-increasing crisis of health and well-being need within society.

What is needed:

There is a growing need to understand people who struggle mentally and emotionally. If our bodies can be broken at times, so can our minds. It is easy for us to brush off worries and anxieties without fully engaging with the people who struggle. The Bible addresses anxiety, fear and worry and gives an indication of the answer in God – see, for example, Matthew 6:25-34. In particular we are told very clearly what to do in this scripture: 'Do not be anxious about anything, but in every situation, by prayer and petition, with thanksgiving, present your requests to God. And the peace of God, which transcends all understanding, will guard your hearts and your minds in Christ Jesus' (Philippians 4:6-7). I've tried to apply this in my own life, but putting it into practice is easier said than done. Nevertheless, faith is important, but helping those who suffer also requires compassion and pastoral sensitivity.

All of us will have encountered someone who has struggled with some difficult experiences. It may even be the person reading this paragraph right now – you. An openness in prayer with God is vital if we are to see people filled with God's love and restoring power. Wisdom and tact, teaching and compassion are essential ingredients to finding breakthrough for those that struggle.

Engaging and understanding:
As we prepare ourselves to pray for all who struggle or who face overwhelming situations that result in mental and emotional health issues, ask God to soften your heart, and be prepared to listen.

Don't have instant answers. People who are overwhelmed sometimes feel ashamed and struggle in their mind and emotions. They can appear distant and withdrawn. Those suffering need to have safe places and trusted people to turn to. Whether praying with individuals or in groups, there is a need for confidentiality and great wisdom. Needs shared and prayed about will require confidentiality, discretion and compassion.

While there are useful methods or techniques for coping, a prayerful approach should avoid pressure or being overly directive. Prayerfully develop sensitivity and the ability to listen to people, and to the Holy Spirit. Be aware that praying for people who are suffering with fear, anxiety, torment and brokenness will be challenging but rewarding as we move out in faith. God's desire is to heal and restore those who suffer.

Patrick Regan OBE encouraged everyone in the summer of the 2020 Covid-19 pandemic to 'Be gentle with yourself your're [sic] doing the best you can. Your best is good enough, go gently'.[51] During the August 2020 holiday period he was emphasising the need for care and compassion for one's self as well as others. As you call upon God for those who need his intervention, remember to include yourself! Jesus told us of the importance of loving others as you love yourself (Mark 12:31). That should guide and temper our approach.

These are also useful scriptures to remember:

> the LORD is compassionate and gracious, slow to anger, abounding in love.
> (Psalm 103:8)

> A gentle answer turns away wrath, but a harsh word stirs up anger. The tongue of the wise adorns knowledge, but the mouth of the fool gushes folly.
> (Proverbs 15:1-2)

The practicalities:

Research which is regularly done nationally shows annual increases, with recent figures showing currently that a quarter of people in the country are likely to have some kind of mental health problem each year, and that a fifth of the population will experience anxiety and depression every week.[52] Symptoms experienced by sufferers are very practical. The most severe cases will experience a number of these things – hyperactivity, loss of sleep, phobias, depression, oppression, heaviness, obsessive compulsive disorder (OCD), post-traumatic stress disorder (PTSD), bipolar or some other conditions. More commonly, people are generally anxious and nervous due to the pressures of life experiences, upbringing and unexpected events.

Keys to effectiveness:

Effective prayer for those struggling with mental health issues comes from compassion and understanding. Understanding symptoms and causes helps, but prayer requires spiritual discernment and application of Scripture. Here are some key areas to consider:

- *Cause and effect.* The experiences of life's relationships can leave a mark, both positive and negative: 'Do to others as you would have them do to you' (Luke 6:31).
- *How people are treated.* Words matter, particularly in how they are spoken: 'The tongue has the power of life and death, and those who love it will eat its fruit' (Proverbs 18:21).
- *Shock experiences.* Life is full of surprises. Some experiences come as a shock in timing and circumstance and affect us deeply: 'Dear friends, do not be surprised at the fiery ordeal that has come on you to test you, as though something strange were happening to you' (1 Peter 4:12).
- *Fight and flight:* Internal defences kick in naturally within our body when faced with deep anxiety. For some people, the result can be excessive panic, irrational thoughts and unpredictable behaviour that extends beyond normal boundaries: 'So do not fear, for I am with you; do not be dismayed, for I am your God. I will strengthen you and help you; I will uphold you with my righteous right hand' (Isaiah 41:10).
- *Grief and getting closure.* Everyone will grieve when experiencing loss. Finding short-term comfort helps, but long-term acceptance is essential, although closure is not something to be rushed: 'Surely he took up our pain and bore our suffering, yet we considered him punished by God, stricken by him, and afflicted' (Isaiah 54:3).
- *Self-worth and* value. When we experience hardship, doubts can come that will affect our confidence: 'I praise you because I am fearfully and wonderfully made; your works are wonderful, I know that full well' (Psalm 139:14).
- *Coping with failure.* If we have failed, think we have failed or have let others down, we are facing one of the most difficult

of life's experiences. Coming to terms with this is difficult but not impossible: 'My flesh and my heart may fail, but God is the strength of my heart and my portion for ever' (Psalm 73:26).

- *Dealing with unfaithfulness and disappointments.* People let us down, and this results in mistrust and caution. 'When I am afraid, I put my trust in you. In God, whose word I praise – in God I trust and am not afraid. What can mere mortals do to me?' (Psalm 56:3-4).

- *When our trust is violated.* Sometimes people can overstep the mark and take too much for granted: 'Do nothing out of selfish ambition or vain conceit. Rather, in humility value others above yourselves' (Philippians 2:3).

- *The aftermath of abuse.* Sadly, people's lives are shattered by inappropriate behaviour and the result can be torment and bad dreams: 'He heals the broken-hearted and binds up their wounds' (Psalm 147:3).

- *Recovery from trauma.* People are deeply affected by an unexpected death or event. During the Covid-19 pandemic of 2020, this was particularly poignant. 'So do not fear, for I am with you; do not be dismayed, for I am your God. I will strengthen you and help you; I will uphold you with my righteous right hand' (Isaiah 41:10).

Activation

Biblical perspective:

Therefore, I urge you, brothers and sisters, in view of God's mercy, to offer your bodies as a living sacrifice, holy and pleasing to God – this is your true and proper worship. Do not conform to the pattern of this world, but be transformed by the renewing

of your mind. Then you will be able to test and approve what God's will is –his good, pleasing, and perfect will.
(Romans 12:1-2)

The weapons we fight with are not the weapons of the world. On the contrary, they have divine power to demolish strongholds. We demolish arguments and every pretension that sets itself up against the knowledge of God, and we take captive every thought to make it obedient to Christ.
(2 Corinthians 10:4-5)

The thief comes only to steal and kill and destroy; I have come that they may have life, and have it to the full.
(John 10:10)

Prayer points:
How and what do we pray, then? The scriptures above really help to bring some focus when it comes to understanding the battle of the mind and the need to get the right kind of help and guidance. Here are some prayer points to focus on. Pray for those struggling that

- they would know that God loves them unconditionally: 'But God demonstrates his own love for us in this: while we were still sinners, Christ died for us' (Romans 5:8);
- there is hope for getting through worry and anxiety as we learn how to give it to the Lord: 'Cast all your anxiety on him because he cares for you' (1 Peter 5:7);
- there is the promise of sleep for God's 'beloved': 'In vain you rise early and stay up late, toiling for food to eat – for he grants sleep to[a] those he loves' (Psalm 127:2);

- they can trust God and he will never let them down: 'Trust in the LORD with all your heart and lean not on your own understanding' (Proverbs 3:5);

- by presenting requests to God, he will bring peace: 'Do not be anxious about anything, but in every situation, by prayer and petition, with thanksgiving, present your requests to God. And the peace of God, which transcends all understanding, will guard your hearts and your minds in Christ Jesus' (Philippians 4:6-7);

- there is healing for the broken-hearted: 'He heals the broken-hearted and binds up their wounds' (Psalm 147:3);

- failure is not the end for anyone; God will strengthen them: 'My flesh and my heart may fail, but God is the strength of my heart and my portion for ever' Psalm 73:26;

- where there is grief, God will bring his comfort. 'Blessed are those who mourn, for they will be comforted (Matthew 5:4);

- when feeling undervalued, they are fearfully and wonderfully made: 'I praise you because I am fearfully and wonderfully made; your works are wonderful, I know that full well' (Psalm 139:14);

- even when having bad experiences, the Lord will strengthen them: 'I can do all this through him who gives me strength' (Philippians 4:13);

- following stress and trauma, that effects of shock will not remain deeply rooted;

- when memories return, that they won't reawaken stress or feelings of being weighed down.

Application:
Our churches can be a safe place and a refuge for people who have gone through trauma and bad experiences. Those who worry and are fearful need to be welcomed and loved, and to know that they will not be rejected and cast aside. Although you may sometimes feel drained by those who are depressed, it is an opportunity to bring the love and presence of Jesus to them, in faith. Those who are downcast need to know they can have 'hope and a future' (Jeremiah 29:11). There are many ways to offer faith-filled strategies to teach, encourage and disciple. For example, 2 Corinthians 10:5 speaks of 'demolishing arguments' that can operate in people's minds, and taking thoughts 'captive', and Romans 12:2 tells us: 'Do not conform to the pattern of this world, but be transformed by the renewing of your mind. Then you will be able to test and approve what God's will is – his good, pleasing and perfect will' – emphasising sound teaching.

Together with regular prayer, offer:

- discipleship through one-to-one mentoring;
- Christian counselling[53] strategies;
- informal Christian resources such as run by Kintsugi Hope[54] (well-being groups);
- friendship groups, home groups, Bible studies, etc.

Sufferers of depression and those who have a rollercoaster of mental and emotional experiences will need consistent, faithful and unswerving support. The Church is a great place to create a safe oasis that can lead to healing, peace, and restoration. Prayer with sensitively and understanding is a great starting point for the church family.

Testimony:

I have had an amazing rollercoaster life of adventure, full of music and creativity. My Christian upbringing gave me a great moral grounding, and my life was full of interesting experiences. I lost my way as a young adult, experiencing failure academically and relationally. However, God recaptured my heart. I found his path again, and will be forever grateful for the grace that has helped me to be faithful, consistent and more secure in my marriage and family life. I also had stimulating jobs, church leadership and the privilege of seeing God at work in his people. By that point I was an associate pastor. Then in 2001 the unthinkable happened. My pastor, best friend and mentor collapsed and died very suddenly. Shock and grief struck me and the whole church.

I was quickly thrust into senior leadership; there was complete change everywhere. I helped everyone through their grief but neglected my own. I nearly had a nervous breakdown. I lost my 'song' (in other words, my desire to sing and worship) for six months. I felt traumatised, frozen emotionally and was joyless. It was like nothing I had experienced before. The psalmist speaks of this very well here: 'Relieve the troubles of my heart and free me from my anguish' (Psalm 25:17).

Then breakthrough came. I was reading the Psalms and felt led to declare them aloud; it came deep from within my heart. I visited a counsellor friend, explained what had happened, and he was relieved for me, as he had been worried. Over the next few months my desire to sing out songs of worship returned, and joy was restored. I praise God for his faithfulness. I have memories of this time and they help me to be compassionate and understanding towards people who are depressed.
Roger Grassham

Prayer/Action:

Dear Lord, I ask you to fill my heart with compassion and understanding for those who struggle with fear and anxiety. I ask that you lift depression from those who have had traumatic experiences. Will you heal them and restore their souls? In Jesus' name. Amen.

Quote:

Were he writing today, Paul might add, 'neither depression, nor anxiety, nor self-harm; no pain from the past or the present or the future; no disappointment or shattered dream, can stop God from loving us.'

Patrick Regan[55]

Guide 17

How to: Pray regarding financial pressure and provision

Preparation

The aim:

This guide aims to help when praying for the financial issues that affect our lives. Everyone needs money to live. At some point every person will need to deal with monetary pressure. There is also a need to understand how to steward what we have. This guide does not set out to address the question of how to handle money from a professional point of view. However, there is a need to know what the Bible has to say so that we can pray effectively and fervently (see James 5:16, KJV) about the financial matters that affect everyone. Also, we do need to know how to navigate deficit and surplus money, both from a spiritual and practical standpoint! This guide addresses our attitude towards finance, so that we can better handle pressures and provision.

What is needed:

Having money to pay our way is a basic need. It is the currency of earth just as faith is the currency of the spiritual world. Commonly people will work to have the finance to pay bills and live. There is a huge variety of types of work, but it should all generate income. For some it is barely enough, but for others it can provide a surplus of disposable income. In each case wisdom is needed in how to spend and invest money wisely. The nation's economy is founded upon principles that enable businesses to be started that provides goods or services. Most succeed, but others fail, resulting in stress on people's finances. Sadly, people are made redundant for various reasons.

Where people are unable to work, the welfare system set up by governments helps to provide the basics. In the worst circumstances, people lose everything and find themselves in poverty on the streets. In 2020, the Covid-19 pandemic had a huge impact on the economy and as a result, people experienced increased financial hardship and redundancy, resulting in unprecedented worry and anxiety in society as a whole.

Knowing what the Bible has to say about money is a good starting point in preparing to pray about all things financial.

Engaging and understanding:
We need to have a clear understanding of several important governing factors that give a Christian context about finance and some foundational truths about its use.

a) Disciples of Jesus are stewards of everything God provides for us, which includes our money: 'Each of you should use whatever gift you have received to serve others, as faithful stewards of God's grace in its various forms' (1 Peter 4:10). See also Luke 14:28; 1 John 3:17.

b) We are not to love money, as it will steal our hearts. We are to be content, knowing that as we learn to love God and walk in the ways of his Word, he will guide us into the abundance of his resources: 'Keep your lives free from the love of money and be content with what you have, because God has said, "Never will I leave you; never will I forsake you"' (Hebrews 13:5). See also Ecclesiastes 5:10; Matthew 6:21.

c) We are to be generous with money and understand that in giving it opens the door for more of God's provision: 'Give, and it will be given to you. A good measure, pressed down, shaken together and running over, will be poured into your lap. For with the measure you use, it will be measured to you' (Luke 6:38). See also Proverbs 19:17.

d) We are exhorted to tithe. This is a principle that is constant throughout the Bible, and which is to do with honouring the Lord, and the attitude of our heart: 'Honour the LORD with your wealth, with the firstfruits of all your crops' (Proverbs 3:9). See also Malachi 3:8; 2 Corinthians 9:6-8.

e) God provides for what we need. This thought should focus thinking on God's priorities and is a direct challenge to greed and selfishness. When he sees our good stewardship, he trusts us with more. 'For where your treasure is, there your heart will be also' (Matthew 6:21). See also Matthew 25:14-30.

f) God does not want us to be idle. He wants us to have a good work ethic. Having a mind to work is a scriptural concept (particularly to be found in Nehemiah 4:6): 'Laziness brings on deep sleep, and the shiftless go hungry' (Proverbs 19:15). See also Proverbs 14:23; 2 Thessalonians 3:1-11.

The practicalities:
There are wide-ranging perspectives about finance in the Christian Church. These can vary from the need to live frugally on the one hand to promoting wealth on the other. This prayer guide is hopefully based on a balanced perspective, seeking to present scriptural ways in which needs and provision are met. Our prayers should consider real-life issues. As we prepare our hearts to pray effectively, here are some practical factors to have in mind.

Fears about:
- running out of money and the consequences of not being able to pay bills;

- getting into debt, and the shame we can feel if we do;
- whether faith will enable God to meet needs, as said in Scripture;
- whether a job is going to be there in the future;
- whether the economy will go into recession, and the affects;
- what will happen if someone steals money from us;
- coping because we are in receipt of benefits and are in poverty;
- spending to support addictions; for example, gambling, drugs, drink, etc.

Responsibilities:
- wanting to make sure all the rent, mortgage and other bills get paid for ourselves/ family;
- wanting to do an effective job at work so that our financial future is secure;
- wanting to plan longer term, especially the need to have enough for retirement;
- wanting to ensure that money is invested wisely;
- wanting to spend money wisely and keep within our means;
- employing staff and wanting to establish and grow businesses to God's glory.

Generosity to people:
- wanting to know how much we should give to the church;
- wanting to know how much we should give away to others;
- wanting to know which are the right financial priorities.

Keys to effectiveness:

It important to remember that we as Christians are people of faith as well as needing to be wise stewards of what God has provided for us. Our attitude towards finance will reflect our trust in God, and the priorities in our heart. Some keys to effective prayer about finance will include building a 'bank' of values:

- *faithfulness* to God in everything he has provided for us;
- *generosity* as an underlying value that enables us to respond to needs;
- *tenderness of heart* that allows us to have a compassionate response to needs;
- *self-control* when faced with temptation to spend unwisely;
- *integrity* in all financial transactions as we pursue righteous acts;
- *perseverance* in trusting God when financial difficulties arise;
- *understanding* that provision comes from the Lord as we depend on him and walk in his ways;
- *decisions* about financial affairs will be made with care, knowing God's priorities;
- *wisdom* when making financial decisions for loans and large expenditure.
- *stewardship* when supervising the handling of finance, with an emphasis on responsibility, governance and when to be generous, by faith.

Activation

Biblical perspective:

And my God will meet all your needs according to the riches of his glory in Christ Jesus.
(Philippians 4:19)

Give, and it will be given to you. A good measure, pressed down, shaken together and running over, will be poured into your lap. For with the measure you use, it will be measured to you. (Luke 6:38-39)

As Jesus looked up, he saw the rich putting their gifts into the temple treasury. He also saw a poor widow put in two very small copper coins. 'Truly I tell you,' he said, 'this poor widow has put in more than all the others. All these people gave their gifts out of their wealth; but she out of her poverty put in all she had to live on.' (Luke 21:1-4)

Prayer points:
The scriptures above help bring some focus; for example, God's provision, and generosity in giving to those in need. Let us pray for:

- provision for those who are trusting God regarding their financial pressure;
- God's intervention for those who are in debt and facing financial ruin;
- a job for those who have been made redundant;
- speedy resolution for those who have discovered money stolen from their bank;
- God's guidance to know how to give to need, and how much;
- employers to be full of integrity and to be fair to their staff;
- those who are on benefits to be without shame, and to know God's love and care;
- those who struggle to return to work following a long layoff;
- individuals and families to have enough to meet their needs;
- Christians to have faith in God's provision in the face of challenges in the economy.

The 2007-2008 financial crisis and the Covid-19 pandemic in 2020 are case in points about unexpected financial challenges affecting individuals, families and the nation as a whole.

Application:
Everyone will face challenging financial circumstances at some point in their life. Some Christians will struggle to apply faith, and tend to depend on their own ways of solving problems. The true way God has provided for his disciples is one of trust and faith in what he can and wants to provide. Being good stewards with what we have and to be willing to give as God leads are two major principles of faith. It is important to understand that God wants to provide for all his creation, but some people in our world have challenging situations. Although they don't want to live in poverty, their life experiences restrict what is possible. Many people experience financial need, but still trust God to provide for them. The value of money and the standards of living vary from country to country. Regardless of our situations, God wants us to be generous and to give, and to trust him as we do so. Whether we have sufficient or little available finance, a willingness to give is both a scriptural and practical principle.

- In the Luke 6:38-39 passage above, the teaching is the same as the teaching in Galatians 6:7-9 about the law of the harvest: what you sow you reap. With whatever God has provided us (either large or small), as we give, God gives back to us.
- In the Luke 21:1-4 passage above, the widow only had two coins and gave them both. The rich gave a larger sum, but Jesus pointed out that the widow had given more, because she had given all she had. Her trust and faith was deeper, in this illustration; she knew in doing this that she activated God's promise to meet her every need.

The application of these principles in life and in prayer applies to everyone, whatever their financial circumstances.

There are some sources of help available within the body of Christ for debt and money management. In the UK, John Kirkby started the charity Christians Against Poverty (CAP), which has a great programme to help people out of debt.[56] In the US, Gary Keesee Ministries (Forward Financial Group) offers both debt advice and also money management and investment.[57]

Testimony:

The CAP website has many stories of people struggling with debt and how their lives have been transformed and changed by connecting with this ministry. Many people have come for help having had no church and faith background. However, through the loving and caring way they have been treated, they have been impacted by the gospel, as well as be given sound financial guidance. See https://capuk.org/our-impact/life-changing-stories.[58]

All of us will have a story about God's provision.

On a number of occasions during our time in pastoral ministry, my wife, Ros, and I have been prompted to give sums of money to individuals, and to charities. On one occasion, our young people were going to a summer youth camp and had to unexpectedly hire a minibus because our own had broken down. At that time, we had several costly expenses ourselves. We decided to trust God and give £250 to help cover the costs for the hire vehicle. Within the following week I received a cheque in the post for the exact amount we had given away! How amazing is our God! This has happened many times, so we have proved you cannot out give God.

Roger Grassham

Remember, 'faith comes from hearing' (Romans 10:17). There is nothing like hearing practical financial stories of God's intervention. It builds faith and stimulates prayer.

Prayer/Action:

Dear Lord, I ask for your sovereign intervention in my life. I ask for you to meet my financial situation. By faith I trust you to 'meet all [my] needs according to the riches of [your] glory' (Philippians 4:19). Thank you for hearing my heart's cry. In Jesus' name. Amen.

Quote:

Money never stays with me. It would burn me if it did. I throw it out of my hands as soon as possible, lest it should find its way into my heart.
John Wesley[59]

4. Different Styles of Prayer[60]

Agreement

This is when two or more people pray together in faith, believing for the same thing, and the same result. When we are living in obedience to the Word of God and our prayers are in line with Scripture, we can join with someone else and pray in unity about the same matter. It is also an 'agreement' with God's Word relating to our lifestyle as well as our prayers.

Confession

The Lord will always hear our heart's cry. When we know that we have let God down by our wrong thoughts or actions, he does not lock us out, but waits for us to turn again to him, confess our sins, our faults and our failings. He is always ready to forgive our repentant heart and restore us as we renew our walk with him. When God forgives, he forgets: 'I, even I, am he who blots out your transgressions, for my own sake, and remembers your sins no more' (Isaiah 43:25).

Contemplation

Contemplative prayer is a time when we centre our full attention on the presence of God over an extended period of time. It means thoughtfully considering the importance of God's will, his love and his Word. We come before the Lord in this way to see him with the eyes of our heart, and then wholeheartedly worship him. As we open ourselves to God in contemplation, we enter into the prayer of the heart.

Intercession

What a privilege God has given us that we can come before him, get really close to him and begin to plead on behalf of another's need. Our intervention on someone's behalf is what our Saviour, Jesus, does when he represents us before the Father's throne and intercedes for us (Hebrews 7:25). We join with him when we intercede for others.

Petition

When we petition God, we are formally and seriously bringing heartfelt prayers to God in the earnest hope that he will intervene on someone's behalf. Just as good parents long to give good gifts to their children, so our heavenly Father desires to give good gifts to his children (Matthew 7:11). He also knows how to develop our lives so that he brings out the best in us. However, James 4:2 tells us: 'You desire but do not have ... You covet but you cannot get what you want, so you quarrel and fight. You do not have because you do not ask God.' We need to make our requests known to him. So, understanding the serious matter that concerns us is directly linked with the attitude of our hearts, and the need for unity.

Praise

We need to give honour to our Lord and praise him for who he is, not only for what he has done. Jesus' death and resurrection is the foundation of everything that is available to us. Our thanks and praises are what we can give him that come from us and cost him nothing. Everything the Lord has done has come from his unconditional love and mercy and not to gain our thanks and praise. That is our gift to him. We should also understand that often praise is an act of the will, as life can be full of challenging circumstances. When we praise God whatever our situation, it releases the power of God because we are affirming God's will over our own.

Thanksgiving

As we come into God's presence, we need to come with thanksgiving, and with gratitude for all that he is, and all that he has done. Without the blood of Christ, we would not be able to come into the Lord's presence at all (Hebrews 9:22). We should thank him for his unfailing loving-kindness for us, praising him that he is just and merciful (Matthew 5:7).

Worship

We need to ask ourselves – does the Lord have first place in our lives? Many people may no longer worship gods of wood and stone, but they have been replaced by giving first place to money, power or fame, among other things. Even worthy matters can demand our time and attention and therefore take first place in our lives. Our Lord and God alone is worthy of our worship and worthy of having the first place and the very best of our lives. Let us honour God by reverencing him at all times and giving him all of our adoration, and doing it with our whole heart instead of just a part of it.

5. Our Responsibilities in Prayer[61]

The following are key scriptures that are clear instructions that remind us of our prayer responsibilities. When you look at the verses, you will see that there is an 'imperative' to do what is being said. In other words, there is a sense of urgency about something which needs to be understood and acted upon. If we take these scriptures seriously, and follow through what they require of us, we will reap the fruit of it. I have put at the end of each scripture the 'outcomes' we can expect if we are obedient to God's Word here.

1. Pray for the *leadership of a nation* that they may find the good and right way to lead: 'As for me, far be it from me that I should sin against the LORD by failing to pray for you. And I will teach you the way that is good and right' (1 Samuel 12:23).
   Outcome: God will teach us the way that is good and right.

2. We need to pray that *we will have godly desires*: 'Take delight in the LORD, and he will give you the desires of your heart' (Psalm 37:4).
   Outcome: The desires of our heart follow obedience.

3. Pray that the city of *Jerusalem will become like its name that means 'City of Peace'*: 'Pray for the peace of Jerusalem: "May those who love you be secure"' (Psalm 122:6).
   Outcome: We will have security.

4. Pray that *the Lord will make Jerusalem a city to be praised*: 'and give him no rest till he establishes Jerusalem and makes her the praise of the earth' (Isaiah 62:7).
   Outcome: Jerusalem will be the praise of the earth.

5. We must pray for *those who mistreat us*: 'bless those who curse you, pray for those who ill-treat you' (Luke 6:28).
   Outcome: 'Your reward will be great' (Luke 6:35)

6. Pray *for labourers to bring in the harvest*: 'A man in the crowd called out, "Teacher, I beg you to look at my son, for he is my only child' (Luke 9:38); 'He told them, "The harvest is plentiful, but the workers are few. Ask the Lord of the harvest, therefore, to send out workers into his harvest field' (Luke 10:2).
   Outcome: Reaping the harvest.

7. We need to pray that *we do not enter into temptation*: 'On reaching the place, he said to them, "Pray that you will not fall into temptation"' (Luke 22:40).
   Outcome: Deliverance from evil (Matthew 6:13)

8. Pray that *we may do no evil*: 'Now we pray to God that you will not do anything wrong – not so that people will see that we have stood the test but so that you will do what is right even though we may seem to have failed' (2 Corinthians 13:7).
   Outcome: We do what is right.

9. Pray that *our love may abound towards all people*: 'And this is my prayer: that your love may abound more and more in knowledge and depth of insight' (Philippians 1:9).
   Outcome: More love will be evident.

10. Pray and *make needs known* with thanksgiving: 'Do not be anxious about anything, but in every situation, by prayer and petition, with thanksgiving, present your requests to God' (Philippians 4:6).
    Outcome: The peace of God will come (Philippians 4:7)

11. Pray that *God will open doors for ministry of the Word*: 'And pray for us, too, that God may open a door for our message, so that we may proclaim the mystery of Christ, for which I am in chains' (Colossians 4:3).

    Outcome: Preaching 'in season and out of season' (2 Timothy 4:2)

12. Pray *to be kept by the power of God*: 'May God himself, the God of peace, sanctify you through and through. May your whole spirit, soul and body be kept blameless at the coming of our Lord Jesus Christ' (1 Thessalonians 5:23).

    Outcome: Being 'shielded by God's power' (1 Peter 1:5)

13. Pray for *national and local leaders of government*: 'I urge, then, first of all, that petitions, prayers, intercession and thanksgiving be made for all people – for kings and all those in authority, that we may live peaceful and quiet lives in all godliness and holiness' (1 Timothy 2:1-2).

    Outcome: We live in peace and quietness.

6. Praying as Jesus Taught Us

When the disciples asked Jesus to teach them to pray, he gave them what we call the Lord's Prayer.[62] It is really the Disciples' Prayer – the prayer pattern that the Lord gave his followers as an example of how to pray.

Here are some suggestions regarding how to follow the pattern that Jesus gave us.

In this manner, therefore, pray:
'Our Father in heaven,
Hallowed be Your name.
Your kingdom come.
Your will be done
On earth as it is in heaven.
Give us this day our daily bread.
And forgive us our debts,
As we forgive our debtors.
And do not lead us into temptation,
But deliver us from the evil one.
For Yours is the kingdom and the power and the glory
forever.
Amen.'
(Matthew 6:9-13, NKJV)

Our Father

As we say these words, we acknowledge that every Christian, whatever their nationality, culture, ethnic background or social standing is part of our 'family'. In Christ, we are one family and come to God as our Father. Many people's experience of 'father' may not have been positive, but our heavenly Father can be trusted, is pure and just. *Thank God that we are part of his family.*

… in heaven

This reminds us that we are coming to a God who is not bound by any of our earthly limitation of time and sense, but that he is eternal, all-knowing, all-powerful, and all-wise. *Praise God that he is perfect and that he loves us.*

… hallowed be your name

Our God is a holy God and desires that we become like him and live a holy life. As we reverence him and honour him, we will draw closer to him and want to be holy, as he is. Being holy is not being religious but becoming like our Lord so that people see his character being expressed in and through us. We recognise that there is power in Jesus' name. At his name everyone should bow their knee. We should do it now, and join those already in heaven, but we certainly will have to in eternity (Philippians 2:9-11). *Praise him that he is holy, eternal, wise and loving and that we can come into his presence because Jesus shed his blood.*

… your kingdom come

When thinking of God's kingdom, do we think only of an eternal future kingdom where sin and evil will be no more? Where, joy of joys, we will be with the Lord forever and leave behind this world and all its pressures? Rather, Jesus is telling us we can have his kingdom now, in our hearts and daily expressed in our lives. When we see God bringing salvation, healing and deliverance to people's lives as we pray, the kingdom of God is clearly revealed right here, right now. *Pray that his kingdom rule will become part of our lives, our family's lives, in our communities and in our nation.*

… your will be done, on earth as it is in heaven

Is it possible to have a place without sin and evil on this earth? That would indeed be heavenly. As we walk closely with God, heaven will be in our hearts no matter what our circumstances. As we learn to love and be obedient to our Lord and Saviour, we will have a taste of heaven in our hearts that will become evident to others around us. To love the Lord our God with all our heart and our neighbour as ourselves is the heart of God's Word – see Matthew 22:36-39. *Let us pray that our lives, our families, our communities and our nations will become obedient to the will of God.*

Give us today our daily bread

We all have needs and Jesus reminded us that as he provided for the birds, so he will provide for our daily needs (Luke 12:24). It is a challenge to our fearful hearts to trust him without anxiety. As we walk closely with God, our daily bread will be practical and spiritual. He will provide nourishment for our physical and soul's needs. *Thank him for the blessings of each day. His blessings are new every morning.*[63]

And forgive us our debts …

How often we ask God to forgive us for our sins, our faults and our failings. Being sorry is not enough. It is possible that Judas was sorry he had betrayed the Lord, although we will never know. However, he did not repent. Remorse may be felt by an individual, but it is not necessarily repentance; it can be regret, which leads to no restorative action. When we ask God for forgiveness, let there be repentance that leads to a change of thinking in the way we live. *Pray that the Lord will help us to renew our minds,*[64] *the way we think, so that we become more like him.*

… as we also have forgiven our debtors

Yes, people will hurt and wound us; some will do so deliberately, and others without realising what they have done. It is more important to have a forgiving heart than to hold on to the hurt. Forgiveness is not easy. Sometimes we need to ask the Holy Spirit to help us. Having a desire to forgive is very important; a forgiving heart keeps the door of God's forgiveness open to their lives. *Pray to have a forgiving heart and bless those who have hurt or wounded you.*

And lead us not into temptation …

How often we struggle with temptation when we should be keeping away from the source of it! Sometimes the circumstances of our lives present us with huge challenges. You might also wonder whether God has allowed the circumstances to challenge our motives and commitment to him. You can be sure that God wants us to resist temptation, and our will needs to be engaged to ensure that this happens. *Let us ask the Lord to help us to stay true to him and keep walking on the right path of obedience to his ways.*

… but deliver us from the evil one

Evil comes, and we cannot divert it – but God can and there are many testimonies of God's deliverance from evil and from danger. I once had real fear when with people in authority that I didn't know. I felt under pressure, afraid of rejection and unsure of how to respond. I was prayed for, for release from fear, and I received real freedom and breakthrough. Rem*ember to ask the Lord for his protection every day.*

for yours is the kingdom …

We must not allow ourselves to be overwhelmed by what we see happening in the world around us, 'for dominion belongs to the LORD and he rules over the nations' (Psalm 22:28). We must always remember to let God be God and never try to usurp his pre-eminent position as Lord of all. *Praise God that beyond what we can see, the Lord's eternal sovereign purposes are being fulfilled.*

... and the power and the glory

We see reflections of power and glory in this world, but they are only small examples of the eternal power and glory of our God and Saviour. We will all have seen people who are hungry for power, and they end up lording it over people. God has ultimate power, but his way was to give us free will to choose him. Now, that is the right way to exercise power and authority; it is the kingdom of God way. As we live our lives, let us always live in a way that gives glory to God and not ourselves. *Praise God that he is all glorious and full of majesty.*

... for ever ...

Our God is eternal. What he has given us through Jesus Christ is eternal and will never fade away.[65] The treasures we lay up in heaven are ours for eternity. The promise of God was to provide a way of salvation so that we, his children, could experience eternity with him. Jesus was God's way. Our acceptance of his lordship and living a life of obedience gives us hope for eternity. *Praise God that he is 'the same yesterday and today and for ever' (Hebrews 13:8).*

Amen

Amen means 'so be it'. Our prayers do not drift around in endless space until 'something' happens. 'In a loud voice they were saying: "Worthy is the Lamb, who was slain, to receive power and wealth and wisdom and strength and honour and glory and praise!"' (Revelation 5:12). When we say Amen, we are effectively saying, 'I agree!' So it is a good idea to always consider very carefully what we say 'Amen' to! *God hears your prayers and values them.*

7. Recommended Reading

There are many books that have been written about prayer. Here are some that I would recommend, and some others that have been recommended by Church leaders. I am sure you will know of others too.

Alistair Cole, *The Dynamics of Effective Prayer* (Merthyr Tydfil: Life Publications, 2008)

E.M. Bounds *The Complete Works of E.M. Bounds on Prayer* (New Kensington, PA: Whitaker House, 2019)

J.C. Ryle, *A Call to Prayer* (Oxford: Benediction Classics, 2017)

Pete Greig, *How to Pray: A Simple Guide for Normal People* (London: Hodder & Stoughton, 2019)

Timothy Keller, *Prayer: Experiencing Awe and Intimacy with God* (Hodder & Stoughton, 2014)

Derek Prince, *Prayer: Shaping History Through Prayer and Fasting* (New Kensington, PA: Whitaker House, 2002)

Philip Yancey, *Prayer: Does It Make Any Difference?* (Grand Rapids, MI: Zondervan, reprint edition, 2016)

Mahesh Chavda: *The Hidden Power of Prayer and Fasting* (Shippensburg, PA: Destiny Image Publishers, 2007)

8. Other Prayer Resources

Elim Pentecostal Church website links with helpful prayer resources:

Prayer for Pentecost – an example prepared in May 2020
www.elim.org.uk/Articles/578726/Join_us_in.aspx

A Day of Prayer – an example prepared in March 2020
www.elim.org.uk/Articles/574156/Prayer_resources_for.aspx

24/7 prayer room ideas
Here is an online link to helpful ideas to assist in the setting up of a designated prayer room.
www.elim.org.uk/Articles/422741/Prayer_Room.aspx

Teachings on prayer
Here are some online links to helpful training audio files that are immediately available.
www.elim.org.uk/Articles/425117/Teaching_on_prayer.aspx

- Confident in the power of prayer
- Confident in the priority of prayer
- Encounter through prayer

9. A Last Word

I don't know about you, but I have found it important to set aside time to listen to what the Lord might want to say to me specifically. So, here I want to share some ideas for personal intercession.

Here is what I do to flow with the Holy Spirit and allow him time to impart deeper understanding, creative thinking, inspirational insight and specific direction in prayer:

1. Find a room or space, indoors or outdoors that I can call my prayer place. For me it's the conservatory in the summer and the lounge in the winter. Sometime my study is a great substitute. At other times I'll go on a familiar walk. If I go for a walk, I'll try to listen to the sounds of nature, look for flowers and wild animals, and if possible, engage all five senses (which might involve taking a snack and drink with me).

2. Sometimes I'll light a candle, look at a picture of a landscape and try to imagine the beauty of God's creation.

3. Other times I'll have worship music playing quietly in the background, either with lyrics or just instrumental. At other times I'll just be quiet and try to still my mind in what is a busy, noisy world.

4. Generally I have a prayer diary and notebook or I'll use my phone or tablet to record notes, either typing or the spoken voice.

5. One final thing is to have my Bible to hand. Over the last decade I've been using search facilities on my phone apps and search engines. However, in the last year I've gone back to my printed, bound Bible, and I've enjoyed the feel of

it in my hands once again. The five senses (sight, sound, smell, taste, touch) are so important to fully engage with God physically, as well as be open to the soul (mind) and spiritual realm.

It would be really helpful if you looked through the prayer guides again, perhaps using one or all of the above approaches. For example, if you use idea 4, you could make notes and record what God might be saying about the people you know who are directly involved.

This devotional approach can be used by an individual, but it can also be used in small groups. What people hear from God by the Holy Spirit as they pray can be noted down then fed back verbally, or passed in writing to whoever might be interested in the outcomes of the intercession. Alternatively, just keep it as part of a prayer diary for that moment in time. You can always come back to it later. I re-read my prayer diaries periodically. By doing this I see where God has answered prayer. It is so encouraging when this happens.

As you prepare yourself to pray, pause between each sentence. Some of the psalms use the word 'Selah' at the end of sections which means, 'Stop and think about that!' Take your time with your prayers and ask the Holy Spirit to help raise your sensitivity levels as you pray, think and reflect. By doing this you are likely to hear God speak. If you do, write down what you hear him say.

Note:
Especially at this time, you may wish to pray the prayer below for all those affected by Covid-19; and, to finish the book, I would like to pray for you, too.

A coronavirus prayer

Father, you know our deep distress about the effects of the coronavirus, worldwide. As we come to our heavenly Father in prayer, we remember that you are our God, who is our 'refuge' and 'strong fortress' (Psalm 31:2).

You are our God and we trust you with our lives and those for whom we are concerned. Help use to always remember to be led by your Holy Spirit and never to be led by a 'spirit of fear',[66] but to embrace your love and power when it is sometimes hard. We acknowledge that when we do this, we will retain a sound mind.

As we unite in prayer, we are reminded that with you, Lord, nothing is impossible. Lord, we ask you to protect us from the spread of coronavirus. But we also ask you to intervene for those who have already been affected. God, we believe that you are the healer. We ask for you to heal those with coronavirus. Lord, have mercy on us. We ask you to restore and renew those whose immune systems have been affected. For those who have underlying health issues, please release healing and transform people by your mighty power through the body of Christ, so that your supernatural work can be seen, and that you will be glorified.

Grant wisdom to our government (wherever we are in the world), also to the World Health Organization, and other leaders as they monitor, assess and lead through this pandemic.

Give strength afresh to all those on the front lines of medicine and health care, the NHS or similar organisations worldwide. In their weariness, enable them to receive your strength, and the alertness and concentration needed, especially in intensive care wards.

Give wisdom and insight to those researching for a long-term cure, and for short-term vaccines. Bring them clear thinking and a breakthrough in all their research and testing.

You are the God who comforts. Embrace those who are grieving the loss of loved ones with your grace. Surround those experiencing trauma and loss, with your compassionate love.

For those in isolation, who are fearful and suffering anxiety, be the 'Prince of Peace' and the 'Wonderful Counsellor'.[67]

You are the God of hope. May we as your people choose hope and faith. May we be beacons of hope and light to those around us.

In this season, may many people come to realise how much you love them. We ask you, Jesus, to reveal yourself as Lord and Saviour to people who are worried, fearful and isolated. May your Church rise up, with wisdom, creativity and compassion. Help us to demonstrate your love in action by practically reaching out to our communities. Lord, please strengthen the countless people who are regularly serving in food banks and delivering to vulnerable people. Keep them safe, and may the recipients be touched by the power of your Spirit as they receive food and other provisions.

We lift our eyes to you, Jesus. You are our helper. Fill us again with your Spirit, with joy and peace as we trust in you. May we overflow with hope by your mighty power. In Jesus' name. Amen.

A prayer for you, the reader

My desire has always been to encourage and equip people to pray more effectively. I personally pray regularly, sometimes conversationally, but always so that I gain greater understanding and focus on what God is trying to say to me in my times of prayer. I have discovered that I can talk to God as if he were walking beside me. This is the same way in which we would walk and talk with our best friend, with respect and time, during which we can listen and pray. I hope you can join me in this journey of deepening intimacy with our heavenly Father, through prayer.

Overall, I sincerely trust you have benefited from reading this book. Here is a prayer I have written especially for you.

Please write your name here: _____

I pray that

Your love for Jesus deepens, and you find fresh insight as you spend time with him.

Your passion for prayer will increase as you open your heart and mind to God.

You have a deep sense of the Lord's presence as you spend time with him regularly.

You will see an increase in your ability to hear the voice of God speaking to you.

You will have dreams and visions from the Holy Spirit to bring revelation to others.

You will receive healing and restoration in areas where you have been hurt.

You find a new heart of worship, even during pressure and responsibility.

You are able to hear God speak even when circumstances present huge challenges.

You experience a surge of faith to fulfil the purposes of God in your generation.

You find peace in the storm, strength to stand up, and faith to speak out.

You have courage and determination, no matter what challenges you face.

You find deep reassurance in the knowledge that with Jesus, you are never alone.

May the peace of Christ dwell in you richly, the hope of God sustains you every day, and the joy of the Lord give you strength even when you don't feel strong in yourself. Remember that God will never leave you nor forsake you,[68] and his power at work in you will never run out. Move forward in faith, and trust God to watch your back for you as you walk with him and obey him every day.

In Jesus' name. Amen.

Endnotes

1. www.prayereleven.org/home/socp/types-of-prayer/ (accessed 2.11.20).

2. Rev Sarah Whittleston is the leader of *Elim Prayer, part of the Elim Pentecostal Church denomination, 2020.*

3. E.M. Bounds, *The Complete Works of E.M. Bounds on Prayer* (New Kensington, PA: Whitaker House, 2019), p. 227.

4. Smith Wigglesworth, ed. Robert Liardon, *On Prayer, Power and Miracles* (Shippensburg, PA: Destiny Image, 2006), Chapter 16, p. 120.

5. Alistair Cole, *The Dynamics of Effective Prayer* (Merthyr Tydfil: Life Publications, 2008), p. 258.

6. Jack Hayford, permission granted from Bridge Logos, Inc. Newberry, Florida for quotes used from *Prayer is Invading the Impossible* by Jack Hayford. ISBN: 9780882708874. www.bridgelogos.com.

7. See for example Matthew 26:41.

8. The Prayer Foundation is part of the ministry of Commonwealth Church in London. www.rodandjulie.com/the-prayer-foundation/ (accessed 31.10.20.

9. John Barr was pastor of the Canning Town Elim Pentecostal Church in east London for twenty-five years, twenty of which I was his assistant/ associate.

10. This refers to Acts 16:9-10 when Paul the Apostle had a vision of a man from Macedonia standing and begging him to come and help them.

11. See for example Matthew 6:9-13.

12. See Acts 8:17. See also Prayer Guide 9.

13. In using 'I' in the book, I represent Elim Prayer as a group of pastoral leaders who together conceived the idea of the Prayer Guides. It has been my privilege to write them all.

14. Psalm 23:1-2.

15. See Hebrews 13:5.

16 C.H. Spurgeon, *The Complete Works of C.H. Spurgeon*, volume 76 (Harrington, DE: Delmarva Publications, Inc., 2015).

17 www.elim.org.uk/Groups/256163/REACH.aspx 2019 (accessed 12.10.19). Edited for use in this book.

18 Reference to 2 Kings 2:13.

19 The website was accessed on 20.10.20.

20 www.gracequotes.org/author-quote/john-calvin/ No 45 (accessed 12.10.20).

21 www.christiansinparliament.org.uk/about/members-stories/lord-rodney-elton/ (accessed 12.10.20).

22 https://quotesthoughtsrandom.wordpress.com/2015/03/04/to-be-a-christian-without-prayer-is-no-more-possible-than-to-be-alive-without-breathing-martin-luther-king-jr/ (accessed 12.10.20).

23 www.elim.org.uk/Publisher/File.aspx?id=228933 (accessed 22.10.20).

24 Dietrich Bonhoeffer, *Life Together* (London: SCM Press, 2015).

25 Limitless is the national youth ministry of the Elim Pentecostal Church, see www.elim.org.uk/Groups/310950/LIMITLESS.aspx (accessed 22.10.20).

26 Limitless Kids is Elim's children's ministry, see www.elim.org.uk/Groups/351695/Limitless_Kids.aspx (accessed 22.10.20).

27 Limitless Youth is Elim's youth ministry, see www.elim.org.uk/Groups/347663/Oxygen_2020.aspx (accessed 22.10.20).

28 https://drlouisehart.com/about/quotes/#:~:text=%E2%80%9CThe%20best%20thing%20to%20spend,first%20step%20towards%20getting%20it.%E2%80%9D (accessed 22.10.20).

29 Prophetic words means something relayed by a Christian inspired by the Holy Spirit. See 2 Peter 1:21

30 From a sermon preached at River Church Canning Town on the subject of 'Hope' on 27.12.14.

31 See 1 Corinthians 12-14.

32 See 1 Corinthians 12:7-11.

33 www.azquotes.com/quote/819600 (accessed 21.10.20).

34 See Mark 16:20.

35 www.smithwigglesworth.com/life/bits.htm (research by the late Des Cartwright, official historian of Elim Pentecostal Churches (accessed 1.11.20)

36 www.christian-quotes.ochristian.com/Holy-Spirit-Quotes/page-11.shtml (accessed 22.10.20).

37 www.crosswalk.com/faith/spiritual-life/inspiring-quotes/31-prayer-quotes-be-inspired-and-encouraged.html (accessed 22.10.20).

38 1 Chronicles 29:11.

39 https://quotefancy.com/quote/908321/Smith-Wigglesworth-When-we-come-to-the-place-of-impossibilities-it-is-the-grandest-place (accessed 12.10.20).

40 See Mark 10:27; Luke 18:27.

41 Sometimes family members get involved in things which have links to the occult, or to organisations that have links to other religions. In those cases, generational curses can affect offspring, albeit not intentional. See Deuteronomy 5:9.

42 www.amazon.com/turning-Charles-Spurgeon-engraved-wooden/dp/B06Y19KG33 (accessed 22.10.20).

43 Joshua 1:3.

44 Alistair Cole, *The Dynamics of Effective Prayer* (Merthyr Tydfil: Life Publications, 2008), p. 210.

45 See for example Jeremiah 2:19; 3:22; 5:6; 15:6; Ezekiel 37:23.

46 'Instead, speaking the truth in love, we will grow to become in every respect the mature body of him who is the head, that is, Christ' (Ephesians 4:15).

47 See 1 Corinthians 12:8-10.

48 www.goodreads.com/quotes/tag/augustine-of-hippo (accessed 12.10.20).

49 Edward Mote (1797-1874), 'My Hope is Built on Nothing Less', https://hymnary.org/text/my_hope_is_built_on_nothing_less (accessed 9.10.20).

50 www.christianheadlines.com/contributors/scott-slayton/encouraging-quotes-about-covid-19-from-christian-leaders.html (accessed 22.10.20).

51 https://twitter.com/patrickregankh/status/1016214586482200576 (accessed 24.10.20).

52 Statistics are widely publicised in the press. These figures are samples that give a broad understanding.

53 See for example www.acc-uk.org; www.faithfulcounseling.com; www.betterhelp.com (accessed 22.10.20).

54 www.kintsugihope.com (accessed 12.10.20).

55 Patrick Regan, *Honesty Over Silence* (Surrey: CWR 2018), p. 154.

56 https://capuk.org/ (accessed 12.10.20).

57 www.garykeesee.com/forward-financial-groups (accessed 12.10.20).

58 Website accessed 12.10.20.

59 www.brainyquote.com/quotes/john_wesley_524898 (accessed 12.10.20).

60 This section is based on helpful teaching by Rev June Freudenberg, which I have adapted.

61 As above.

62 As above.

63 See Lamentations 3:23.

64 Romans 12:2.

65 See 1 Peter 1:4.

66 2 Timothy 1:7, KJV.

67 Isaiah 9:6.

68 Hebrews 13:5.